Tropical North Qld

Atlas & Guide

including Cairns and The Reef

A Hema Outdoor Guide

by Denis O'Byrne

Your guide to a complete Tropical North Queensland experience

Discover Tropical North Queensland

This is the fourth in a series of outdoor guides, published by Hema Maps Pty Ltd and originated by Rob van Driesum. The guides complement the maps that Hema produces, with a focus on outdoor activities.

The Author of this Book

Denis O'Byrne is a freelance journalist and writer currently living in Darwin. He has been writing about travel and the outdoors for more than 25 years and today his work appears in various publications including *RM Williams Outback Magazine* and the national 4WD magazine *Overlander*.

Credits & Thanks

Many people provided assistance and advice during the preparation of this guide and Denis is grateful to them all. Special thanks to Cairns Dive Centre, Peter Hutton, Claire Brophy, Mick & Trish O'Shea, Struan Lamont, Kevin Gilligan, Dan Irby, Terry McClelland, Owen Rankine, Lawrence Mason and Jeremy Little.

Change is Certain

The information presented in this book is always subject to change. Roads change, rules and policies are amended, and new facilities and services spring up while existing ones go out of business. Quoted schedules, prices and contact details were correct at the time of research, but you should always check with operators to avoid disappointment.

This book can only be a guide and should not be taken as gospel. The best advice is to keep an open mind and talk to others as you explore this unique part of Australia – it's all part of the adventure.

Please Tell Us

We welcome and appreciate all your comments and any information that helps us improve and update future editions of this book. Please write to Hema Maps Pty Ltd, PO Box 4365, Eight Mile Plains, Qld 4113, Australia or email manager@ hemamaps.com.au.

Published by

Hema Maps Pty Ltd
PO Box 4365
Eight Mile Plains, Qld 4113
Australia
tel (07) 3340 0000
fax (07) 3340 0099
manager@hemamaps.com.au
www.hemamaps.com
1st edition – June 2005
ISBN-10: 1-86500-303-4
ISBN-13: 978-1-86500-303-0

Copyright

Text & Maps
© Hema Maps Pty Ltd 2005
Photographs
© Photographers as indicated, 2005

Printed by
Fergies, Brisbane

Photographs

Front cover: Beach north of Cairns, Ulysses butterfly, Millaa Millaa Falls, photos courtesy Tourism Queensland. Daisy Cup coral, photo by Viewfinder.

Publisher: Rob Boegheim
Managing Editor: Rob van Driesum
Assistant Editor: Natalie Wilson
Author: Denis O'Byrne
Cartographers: Craig Molyneux, Ross Chrystall
Designer: Debbie Winfield

Contents

Contents

Distinctive Quinkan art at Laura's Split rock gallery.

Introduction

Two outstanding features other than winter sunshine set the Cairns region apart from where most of us live. These are the Great Barrier Reef and the rainforests of the Wet Tropics, both of which are so rich and diverse in life that they've been included on the UN's World Heritage list. They form a solid foundation for a tourism industry that is worth billions of dollars annually.

Most of the outdoor activities on offer between Cardwell and Cooktown in some way involve visits to either the Reef or the forests. Taking visitors on diving and snorkelling trips to view the splendours of the Reef keeps an armada of boats occupied. You can do day, overnight and extended trips, and if you don't hold a dive certificate there are many instructors who'll be delighted to help you get one. If all you want to do is snorkel, you'll find a staggering variety of marine life around the shallower reefs. Numerous small, uninhabited islands lie close enough to the mainland to tempt the kayaker.

Meanwhile, out in the rainforests, people are bushwalking, wildlife-watching, white-water rafting, mountain biking, horse riding, camping and just generally soaking up the cathedral-calm atmosphere of a world of big trees.

Countless waterfalls and cascades plunge down the mountainsides, feeding crystal-clear water holes that are ideal for swimming when stingers close the beaches. You can get a bird's-eye view of this spectacular landscape by taking a flight in a hot-air balloon, hang-glider or light plane, or by doing a parachute jump. Meanwhile, Aboriginal-guided tours allow you to see it through the eyes of the first Australians.

With all the emphasis being placed on the rainforest and Reef, one unique part of the region tends to be forgotten. This is the Atherton Tableland, just an hour or so's drive from Cairns. One of Australia's richest agricultural districts, the Tableland has its own suite of attractions including rainforest, volcanic vents, lakes both large and small, and heritage towns that, unlike their busier coastal neighbours, have retained much of their early character.

Finally, we don't claim that this book lists every outdoor pursuit and every possible venue – you'd need a much thicker, more expensive book to do that. Our hope is that it'll serve to whet your appetite and point you in the right direction when you're planning an activities and nature-based holiday in this truly remarkable part of Australia. ■

Wet Tropics

Great Barrier Reef

Hinchinbrook Island

Licuala State Forest Park

Lake Tinaroo

Great Barrier Reef (soft coral)

Myall Beach

Undara Lava Tubes

Highlights

Far North Queensland has so many diverse attractions that it's difficult to imagine visitors not finding something to enchant them. Who could fail to be captivated by the colours and infinite variety of marine life on the Great Barrier Reef, or the sights and sounds of one of the world's most ancient rainforests?

The following list of highlights is pretty subjective and by no means exhaustive, but it should give you an idea of what to expect. They're listed in the order in which they appear in the book:

- **Wet Tropics.** The rainforests of the Wet Tropics are special places whose spirit touches all who visit them. Go for a walk on any jungle path and soak up the atmosphere of this vibrant green world.
- **Great Barrier Reef.** Go diving or snorkelling or take a glass-bottom boat trip on any pristine reef and marvel at the richness of life that inhabits one of the world's natural wonders.
- **Gillies Hwy.** The seemingly endless twists and turns of this scenic mountain road near Cairns offer an exhilarating drive, particularly for bikers.
- **Hinchinbrook Island.** Take time out to discover the Thorsborne Track, one of Queensland's great walks.
- **Society Flat & Blencoe Falls.** A short rainforest walk at Society Flat, on the road to Blencoe Falls, reveals magnificent kauris and rose gums. The falls are impressive during the dry season and awesome during the Wet.
- **Licuala State Forest Park.** Visit this beautiful grove of tall fan palms near Mission Beach and (with any luck) see cassowaries in the wild.
- **Ella Bay.** Pitch your tent behind the foredune and go for a morning walk on a remote and beautiful beach.
- **Frankland Islands.** Camp out and go snorkelling, bird-watching and kayaking at these five small islands near Cairns.

The Franklands beckon those who crave an island escape without frills.
- **Curtain Fig.** Visit Yungaburra and see one of the region's most remarkable rainforest trees. Wait until the sun goes down and spotlight for nocturnal wildlife.
- **Lake Tinaroo.** Paddle a canoe along the shore and observe local wildlife getting ready to greet the day. Cast a line and (hopefully) catch a barramundi for lunch.
- **Daintree Discovery Centre.** Climb into the forest canopy and wander the boardwalks while learning about the ecology of the Daintree rainforest.
- **Myall Beach.** Get up early and head down to Myall Beach to watch the sun rise over Cape Tribulation and the Coral Sea.
- **Cedar Bay.** One of the Far North's most beautiful beaches is accessible only by foot, boat or seaplane. Take everything you need and spend three or four days – or a week – chilling out in splendid isolation.
- **Chillagoe Caves.** Visit the three show caves for a taste of what other underground delights must be hiding in these ancient coral reefs.
- **Undara Lava Tubes.** Go underground in the world's largest lava tubes and learn how these unique geological features were created.

Orientation

In this book, the term "Far North Queensland" (FNQ) refers to the area from Cardwell north along the coast to Cooktown, and inland as far as Chillagoe and Mount Surprise. Cairns, the region's administrative capital, is roughly halfway between Cardwell and Cooktown, and about 1700km north of Brisbane.

FNQ has a varied geography. In the east are narrow coastal lowlands backed by the rugged Great Dividing Range that, as you head inland, gives way to rolling hills and plains. Tropical rainforests clothe the mountains, while open eucalypt forests and woodlands dominate the drier west. The coastal strip and the Atherton Tableland behind Cairns have largely been cleared for agriculture, and are ranked among Australia's most productive land.

The coastal lowlands and Atherton Tableland are fairly densely settled, with small towns liberally sprinkled over the map. It's a very different story in the sparsely populated west, however, where the climate isn't so conducive to intensive farming. Here you find a land of large cattle stations and tiny isolated communities on the fringes of the Outback.

History

Aboriginal Inhabitants

When European settlers arrived in FNQ in the early 1870s they found the rainforests inhabited by Aboriginal people who had already lived there for thousands of years. Exactly how many thousands of years is unknown, but oral histories of the Atherton Tableland area tell of the volcanic upheavals of 9000 years ago, while archaeologists have determined that a rock shelter near Cairns was in use around 5000 years ago. Countless stone artefacts such as axes, knives and hammer stones have been found in farming areas that were once covered in rainforest. In the west, near Mt Mulligan, occupation sites were being used as long as 35,000 years ago.

As elsewhere in Australia, these people lived in well-organised tribal societies that occupied defined territories in which all landscape features were related to the deeds of ancestral spirit beings. Every person was regarded as being descended from a particular being, which handed down the laws by which that person lived

and whose essence provided his or her life force.

The rainforests between Cardwell and Cooktown were home to around 12 tribal groups. They included the Kuku Yalanji, who occupied the area between present-day Cooktown and Mossman, and the Ngadjonji of the Atherton Tableland. Probably as a result of their environment, these rainforest dwellers were smaller in stature and lighter in skin colour than many other Australian Aboriginal people. Their total population at the time of the British invasion is unknown, but must have numbered in the thousands.

Each tribe, which spoke a distinctive language or dialect, was in turn made up of family-based sub-groups. They lived semi-nomadic lifestyles, their survival dependent on access to a range of resources that could be exploited either on a full-time or seasonal basis. Early White travellers described their semi-permanent wet season camps as having the appearance of villages.

The arrival of European miners and settlers had a devastating impact on the Aboriginal people. In the case of the Ngadjonji, the clearance of their rainforest habitat for agriculture forced them to retreat to rougher areas where they soon began to starve. Conflict between the Ngadjonji and the White settlers around Atherton reached such a height in the mid to late-1880s that the latter demanded the government find some means of placating the Aborigines. In 1889 the Ngadjonji agreed to a truce in which they would cease attacking the settlers if the settlers would provide food and stop attacking them.

Decimated by introduced diseases, deprivation and wholesale slaughter by the settlers, the rainforest tribes were probably reduced to less than 20% of their pre-contact population within 20 years. As European settlement expanded, many of the surviving Aborigines were rounded up and forcibly removed from their ancestral lands to mission reserves at places like Palm Island (off Townsville), Woorabinda (near Rockhampton) and Yarrabah (near Cairns). Under the Aboriginals Protection & Restriction of the Sale of Opium Act (1897), Aboriginal people could be committed to a reserve and held there against their will, with husbands separated from wives and mothers from children. The Act remained in force until 1971.

ROB VAN DRIESUM

The Anglican Church at Yarrabah, the first mission near Cairns and a major Aboriginal town these days

Despite the immense social upheaval of the past 130 years, the rainforest people have managed to hang on to their tribal identities. Today, local Aboriginal culture is on display at the Tjapukai Aboriginal Cultural Park in Cairns and on various Aboriginal-guided tours throughout the region.

European Explorers

The identity of the first foreigners to sight the shores of FNQ is a mystery. Indeed, there is said to be evidence – in the form of buried coins – that Egyptian mariners landed near Cooktown some 2000 years ago. Dutch and Spanish navigators were active around Cape York as early as 1606, and the Chinese and Portuguese may have been there even earlier. However, there is no record of any of them having visited the area in question.

What *is* known is that First-Lieutenant James Cook made the earliest recorded landing here when he careened his ship HMS *Endeavour* near present-day Cooktown to carry out repairs. The ship had struck a reef off Cape Tribulation on 11 June 1770 and it took the crew several weeks to make good the damage. During this time the botanist Joseph Banks busied himself collecting natural history specimens. It was here that *kangaroo* entered the English language.

The next visit of note occurred 74 years after Cook, when the German explorer Ludwig Leichhardt travelled through the region on his epic journey from Brisbane to Port Essington, near today's Darwin. He was attempting (without success) to find a practicable overland route that would help connect Brisbane to the rich markets of Southeast Asia.

The Endeavour River at Cooktown, where Captain Cook repaired his ship in 1770

On 24 May 1848 the English surveyor Edmund Kennedy and 12 companions landed at Tam O'Shanter Point (near present-day Mission Beach) and set off for Cape York. Eventually, after suffering extreme privations, only Kennedy and his Aboriginal guide Jackey Jackey were left to complete the journey. With 30km to go, Kennedy was fatally speared during an Aboriginal attack. Jackey Jackey managed to get to the supply ship waiting at Cape Albany and so entered Australian folklore.

In 1872, the newly formed and cash-strapped colony of Queensland sent William Hann to investigate the southern end of Cape York. Hann found some gold in the Palmer River, but not enough to get excited about. It was the Irish explorer James Venture Mulligan who got the ball rolling the following year when he put 102 ounces of nuggets from the Palmer on public display. So began the legendary Palmer River Gold Rush, one of the richest and wildest of all Australia's rushes. In 1876 Mulligan discovered significant gold deposits in the Hodgkinson River, sparking a new rush that resulted in the founding of Cairns.

European Settlers

In 1873, the closest White settlement to the Palmer River was distant Cardwell. That was no deterrent, however, and Cooktown was soon founded as the new goldfield's administrative and supply centre. It eventually languished, but for a time Cooktown was Queensland's largest town and busiest port after Brisbane.

The discovery of the Hodgkinson River Goldfield brought demands for the establishment of a new port. A route suitable for packhorses was soon found over the ranges from Trinity Inlet, where a settlement called Cairns sprang into existence. However, two years later an easier road – the so-called Bump Track – was found between the Hodgkinson and Port Douglas, which then became the preferred shipping point. Cairns regained the upper hand when it became the port for the Mulgrave Goldfield in 1880.

Four years later Cairns was chosen as the terminus for a new railway to be built over the Kuranda Range to Herberton, a tin-mining centre on the Atherton Tableland. The Tableland was already in the grip of another rush based on 'red gold' – a valuable rainforest hardwood called red cedar. The present-day township of Atherton, which was surveyed in 1885, started out as a logging camp.

Inevitably, it wasn't long before the mining rushes dwindled and the red cedars were cut out. Deprived of their livelihoods, many miners and loggers turned to agriculture. Soon the flatter ground was being cleared for the establishment of sugar cane plantations and dairy farms, and by 1890 sugar was the mainstay of the Cairns economy.

Tourism arrived in the 1920s when the enterprising Hayles family began organising trips from Cairns to the Great Barrier Reef and Green Island. They built the first glass-bottom boats for coral viewing. Around this time Cairns was flattened by a cyclone and rebuilt with concrete and bricks, losing much of its early character in the process.

WWII & After

In 1942 the war in the Pacific was not going well for the Allies. A Japanese invasion of Australia seemed imminent and Cairns, being on the wrong side of the so-called Brisbane Line, was evacuated. Then followed a massive build-up of defence personnel. The Atherton Tableland was turned into a huge training base for American and Australian forces, and Cairns became the major operations and supply base for the war effort in the Southwest Pacific.

Following the war years Cairns returned to its role as a small regional centre servicing the local farming communities. Tourism was still in its infancy, but slowly growing. A local engineer designed and built the world's first underwater observatory, which was installed at Green Island just in time for Queen Elizabeth's visit in 1954.

Cairns's first tourist hotel was built in 1977, and six years later the Japanese invested huge sums in establishing new resorts. Christopher Skase got things moving at Port Douglas in the late 1980s when he built the Mirage Resort. While sugar has waned in recent times, tourism has boomed. Today, Cairns has no sugar mills left operating, but it hosts over two million tourists annually and is the second most popular destination with overseas visitors outside Sydney.

Geology & Landforms

The dramatic ranges along FNQ's coast have their roots in the ancient supercontinent of Gondwana, when mighty rivers carried massive loads of sediment to the sea. Back then – about 400 million years ago – the coastline was located 150km west of where it is today. The coral reefs that formed at that time are now seen as the dramatic limestone outcrops around Chillagoe.

Over time the thick beds of marine sediments were altered by the heat and pressure associated with movements in the Earth's crust. Around 100 million years ago this metamorphic rock, along with underlying granites, was thrust up to form a mighty mountain range. Since then much of the softer metamorphic material has been eroded, but can still be seen as the coastal escarpment. Meanwhile, the more resistant granite forms the high points along today's Great Dividing Range.

A long period of volcanism that only ended about 9000 years ago saw the Atherton Tableland becoming pocked by vents, examples of which can be visited in the Crater Lakes and Hypipamee national parks. During this

Old machinery, Palmer River goldfield

Green Island, a good example of a coral cay

period basaltic lava poured over the countryside, filling valleys and low-lying areas to create the Tableland's distinctive topography. Today, the nutrient-rich basalt soils support complex rainforests and are the basis of a thriving agricultural industry.

The lava flows also filled valleys on the eastern edge of the Tableland. Here the basalt was deeply incised by fast-flowing streams, forming impressive gorges such as those on the Tully and North Johnstone rivers. Waterfalls often mark the upstream limits of erosion in these basalt-filled valleys.

Finally, just as the volcanic age drew to a close, a rise in sea level flooded the coastal lowlands, leaving hilltops standing high and dry to create landforms such as Hinchinbrook, Fitzroy and Snapper islands. These are called "continental" islands. The low sandy type, such as Green Island and the Low Isles, are "cays" formed by a build-up of sand and coral debris on a reef.

The Wet Tropics

Millions of years ago much of Australia was covered by wet tropical rainforest. However, increasing aridity caused its retreat to mostly tiny wetter areas across the north of the continent. By far the largest of these ancient relicts is found along the northeastern coast of Queensland.

At the time of European settlement the wet tropical rainforests of Far North Queensland were much more extensive than they are today. Since the 1870s almost all the rainforest that once covered the coastal lowlands and Atherton Tableland has been cleared, leaving only the more inaccessible areas unscathed. Despite official recognition of its immense conservation value, virgin rainforest was still being logged in the early 1980s. This caused a public outcry that led, in 1988, to 85% of the surviving wet tropical rainforest being placed on UNESCO's World Heritage List.

Ranging in elevation from sea level to 1622m at Mt Bartle Frere, the Wet Tropics of Queensland World Heritage Area covers almost 895,000ha and extends for about 450km along the coast between Townsville and Cooktown. (The tropical rainforest found north of Cooktown is much drier than that further south.)

Bizarre rock colours in an Undara lava tube

The massive prop roots of the coastal pandanus

Cloudy rainforest, here at Crawfords Lookout along the Palmerston Hwy

11

Around 75% of the Wet Tropics is covered by rainforest while the remainder is largely made up of wet sclerophyll forest, dry sclerophyll forest, paperbark swamps and mangrove forests. While most of the WHA is protected within national parks and state forests, a significant portion is owned or leased by a variety of government and private landholders.

The Wet Tropics represents less than a thousandth of the continent's landmass, yet its habitats support 65% of our fern species, 30% of our orchids, 36% of our mammals (including 30% of our marsupial species, 58% of our bats and 25% of our rodents), 50% of our birds, 37% of our freshwater fishes, and 60% of our butterflies. Many of these occur nowhere else.

Also found here are most of the world's surviving relics of the primitive flowering plants, such as the *Proteaceae*, that evolved in the forests of Gondwana. Indeed, 13 of the 19 known primitive families occur here, while only nine are represented in the whole of South America's vast tropical rainforests. Unlike those of Asia, Africa and the Americas, which are of comparatively recent origin, the rainforests of the Wet Topics have an exceptionally high level of endemism due to their great age and long isolation.

With ever-increasing numbers of visitors coming to experience the natural environment, the challenge for managers is to balance their needs and expectations with the requirement to protect the area's intrinsic values. As well as increasing visitor impacts there are several threats to the integrity of the Wet Tropics as a WHA. These include feral animals such as pigs, foxes and exotic fishes; the spread of weeds; wildfires; and incompatible land use – such as cattle grazing – on private property that falls within the Wet Tropics. There is currently a proposal to 'buy back' subdivided land in the Daintree as a means of protecting that area's integrity.

Flora

The Wet Tropics rainforests are home to a staggering 3500 plant species, including over 1000 trees. Two hectares of rainforest can contain 150 species of tree (more than the entire tree flora of Europe) and one tree can have as many as 50 species of epiphyte growing on it.

Not surprisingly, first-time visitors to the rainforest tend to be overwhelmed by the luxuriant green world that crowds around and over them. It takes a little while before you can break the whole down into its component parts and begin to appreciate its complexity. Most interested visitors will soon be able to identify the more obvious species, such as lawyer vines, bird's-nest ferns, red beech, strangler figs, rose gums, kauris and tree ferns. However, without years of study the identity of the vast majority will remain a tantalising mystery.

Rainforest

Rainforest is divided into three major categories based on leaf size – mesophyll (large leaves), notophyll (medium-sized leaves) and microphyll (small leaves). These groups are further

Bird's-nest ferns (left) and basket ferns (top right) are common epiphytes

*The flame tree (*Brachychiton acerifolius, *also known as flame kurrajong) loses its leaves in the Dry and then bursts into bloom, a striking sight*

broken down into 13 structural types related to such factors as altitude, rainfall and soil type.

The most luxuriant and complex rainforests – called mesophyll vine forests – are characterised by an abundance of buttressed trees, strangler figs, thick woody vines (called lianas), palms, epiphytes and fleshy herbs such as ginger. Such forests are found mainly in warm lowland areas with high rainfall and rich soils. The walk to Josephine Falls, in Wooroonooran National Park, takes you through a good example of a complex mesophyll vine forest.

Notophyll vine forests tend to grow on poorer soils in drier, cooler areas. They also have lianas, strangler figs and epiphytes, but tree ferns, lawyer vines and mosses are much more abundant.

Microphyll vine forest grows in the cloudy, wet and windswept highlands such as around the top of Mt Bellenden Ker. The most common type is a simple fern forest in which stunted, moss-covered trees are a major feature. Australia's only native rhododendron is found here.

Buttressed Giants

Some rainforest trees have flattened, plank-like expansions of the surface roots that radiate out from the base. These are called buttresses and can reach heights of 10m.

It's not fully understood what purpose the buttresses serve. To some extent they probably help support a tree's weight in shallow soils. They may also help the trees breathe in waterlogged soils, or enable them to take up nutrients from shallow soils.

There are some impressive buttressed trees along the walking track that leads down to the North Johnstone River from Crawfords Lookout, on the Palmerston Hwy.

Rainforest meets beach at Cape Tribulation

Josephine Falls, set amid complex vine forest

Ginger in Bloom

Mangrove boardwalk near Cairns airport

Wet Sclerophyll Forest

Tall forest dominated by pink bloodwood (*Eucalyptus intermedia*), rose gum (*E. grandis*) and mountain bloodwood (*E. resinifera*) occurs in narrow bands along the western flanks of the rainforest. This forest type grows where you'd normally expect to find rainforest and owes its existence to fire. A good spot to see rose gums is on the Society Flat walking track en route from Cardwell to Blencoe Falls.

Dry Sclerophyll Forest

Found to the west of the rainforest and in rainshadow areas within it are much drier communities dominated by eucalypts. These are essentially open forests or woodlands with a grassy understorey.

Swamplands

Paperbarks (*Melaleuca spp*) dominate poorly drained, low-lying coastal areas where the water table is either above or just below the ground for most of the year. Most of this type of habitat has been drained for agriculture. A good example of a paperbark swamp can be viewed from the Centenary Lakes boardwalk in Cairns's botanic gardens, and you'll see more in the Edmund Kennedy National Park near Cardwell.

Mangroves

With 34 species of mangrove out of 69 worldwide, the Wet Tropics is comparable in terms of species diversity to the world's richest mangrove forests in New Guinea and Southeast Asia. The Wet Tropics includes major mangrove habitats such as the Hinchinbrook Channel and the Daintree River's northern bank. Eleven species can be seen along the mangrove boardwalks near the Cairns airport.

Fauna

A tremendous diversity of animal life is found within the wet tropical rainforest. Many species are endemic to the region, while others also occur in the rainforests of Cape York and New Guinea. A number are considered to be relicts of the ancient fauna of Gondwana.

Mammals

The Wet Tropics is home to 94 species of native mammals including two monotremes, 41 marsupials (10 of which are endemic), 15 rodents (one endemic) and 36 bats. Four of Australia's six species of ringtail possum are endemic to the upland rainforests. Other mammalian rainforest endemics include the musky rat kangaroo and Australia's two species of tree kangaroo.

Despite its small size, the musky rat kangaroo (*Hypsiprymnodon moschatus*) is closely related to kangaroos and wallabies. It's the most primitive member of this family and is thought to represent an early stage of its evolution. The musky rat kangaroo is found at all altitudes in the Wet Tropics, where it eats fruit and small invertebrates. Although its hind feet are longer than its forefeet – like a typical macropod – it gallops rather than hops along when in a hurry. Unlike other native mammals it's active during the day.

Swamp wallaby, commonly known as 'stinker' for its smell

Scrub turkey

Warning sign for tree kangaroos on the Atherton Tableland

Found in forests above 700m, Bennett's tree kangaroo *(Dendrologus bennettianus)* and Lumholtz's tree kangaroo *(D. lumholtzi)* also behave most unlike their macropod cousins. As their names suggest, they live in trees and clamber about quite happily in the forest canopy. All macropods are descended (so to speak) from arboreal ancestors, but at some stage of their evolution they left the trees to live on the ground. Why tree kangaroos returned there is a mystery.

Found in rainforest as well as adjoining open forests and woodland in the Wet Tropics, Cape York and New Guinea, the white-tailed rat *(Uromys caudimaculatus)* grows to about 1kg and lives a largely arboreal existence. It has extremely powerful jaws and enjoys a diverse diet including whatever it can steal from bushwalkers' rucksacks!

Birds

Between them, the Wet Tropics and Great Barrier Reef have a larger number of bird species than any other area of comparable size in Australia. Over 430 species have been recorded, of which around 130 are mainly found in closed forests including mangroves.

The rainforests are home to the region's 12 endemics – the Atherton scrub wren *(Sericornis keri)*; bridled honeyeater *(Lichenostomus frenatus)*; Bowers shrike-thrush *(Colluricincla boweri)*;

The Vanishing Cassowary

The bird that most visitors want to see is the southern cassowary *(Casuarius casuarius)*, a huge, flightless species that inhabits the rainforests of the Wet Tropics, Cape York and New Guinea.

Related to the ostriches of Africa, the kiwis of NZ, the rheas of South America and our very own emus, the cassowary is a relict of the ancient avian fauna of Gondwana. They're remarkable-looking birds with dense, blue-black plumage, raised horny helmets on top of their skulls, pendulous red wattles and bare, bright blue skin on their heads and necks. The helmets and plumage enable them to push quickly through the forest understorey, which often consists of thickets of lawyer vine.

Cassowaries can exceed 2m in height and are heavy, powerful birds. While not generally considered dangerous to humans they can become aggressive if there are chicks about. In the event that you find yourself eyeball to eyeball with one on a jungle track, and the bird doesn't turn and run, you should raise your arms so as to look taller (cassowaries don't have good eyesight), back slowly away and step behind a tree at the first opportunity.

The total population of adult cassowaries left in the wild is estimated to be less than 1500 and falling. Their continuing decline

ROB VAN DRIESUM

is due primarily to the loss of key habitat (mainly lowland forest), collisions with motor vehicles, dog attacks and competition for food from feral pigs. Much of the remaining lowland forest has been subdivided and the need to prevent further land clearing is causing quite a dilemma.

These days the best place to see a cassowary in the wild is the Tam O'Shanter State Forest behind Mission Beach, with the areas around the Lacey Creek and Licuala state forest parks being most reliable – though sightings are still far from guaranteed. If you don't see or hear one (listen for a booming or harsh coughing noise) you'll certainly see where they've been – cassowary droppings are an interesting splattered mash of large fruit seeds and other indigestible plant material.

To learn more about cassowaries, call in to the Wet Tropics Environment Centre, © 07 4068 7179, in Mission Beach. It's next to the visitor information centre on Porter Promenade.

*The green tree python (*Morelia viridis*), not as large as the amethystine python but still a striking sight*

Scrub fowl

Green tree frogs are very common

Ulysses butterfly

chowchilla *(Orthonyx spaldingii)*; fern wren *(Oreoscopus gutturalis)*; golden bowerbird *(Prionodura newtoniana)*; lesser sooty owl *(Tyto multipunctata)*; MacLeays honeyeater *(Xanthotis macleayana)*; mountain thornbill *(Acanthiza katherina)*; pied monarch *(Arses kaupi)*; tooth-billed bowerbird *(Scenopoeetes dentirostris)*; and Victoria's riflebird *(Ptiloris victoriae)*.

Victoria's riflebird is one of the birds of paradise of New Guinea fame, and to see the male's courtship display is a real highlight. The glossy colouration of the golden bowerbird makes it obvious in the dim light of its forest home. At 25cm long it's the smallest bowerbird, but it builds the biggest bower – up to 3m tall.

Other interesting rainforest birds include the scrub turkey *(Alectura lathami)* and orange-footed scrub fowl *(Megapodius reinwardt)*. Both these species are mound builders and have large feet for scratching up the dirt and leaves. The mounds are quite large (up to 5m high in the case of the scrub fowl) and act as incubators for the eggs, which are laid in an excavation in the top of the mound. Rotting vegetation provides the heat source, and the birds maintain the correct temperature by adding or removing leaf litter as required, poking their head in the mound to check.

Most of the birds in the rainforest are heard rather than seen. The wompoo fruit dove *(Ptilinopus magnificus)* is one of the most spectacular fruit doves, but you'll generally only know that it's around by its penetrating "wompoo" or "mollock-woo". There's no mistaking the sharp, whip-crack call of the eastern whipbird *(Psophodes olivaceus)*, or the cat-like wailing of the spotted catbird *(Ailuroedus melanotis)*.

The Wet Tropics has a number of parrots including a subspecies of the crimson rosella *(Platycercus elegans)*, which is restricted to this area. So too is a subspecies of the king parrot *(Alisterus scapularis)*, one of Australia's most beautiful birds.

One of 10 species of kingfisher found here, the buff-breasted paradise kingfisher *(Tanysiptera sylviia)* is easily identifiable by its long white tail and rich blue and chestnut colouration. Part-time residents of New Guinea, the birds migrate to Australia in October/November to breed in the lowland forests of the Wet Tropics and Cape York, where they excavate nest hollows in termite mounds.

Iridescent green Christmas beetle

The golden orb weaver, a magnificent spider named for the colour of its web

Reptiles & Amphibians

The Wet Tropics is home to over 160 reptile species, of which 22 are endemic. Around 20 of the endemics are restricted to rainforest habitats and include one snake, one dragon, three geckoe and 15 skinks. Two of the most interesting lizards are the chameleon gecko (*Carphodactylus laevis*) and the northern leaf-tailed gecko (*Phyllurus cornutus*). Both these large (around 150mm long) geckoe are restricted mainly to the rainforest and are considered primitive species with links to Gondwana.

Reaching a length of 8.5m, the amethystine python (*Morelia amethistina*) is Australia's largest snake. It is another rainforest inhabitant and is most often spotted warming itself in the sun on the forest margins before beginning the day's hunt. The common name refers to the attractive purple iridescence that can be seen on its scales under certain light conditions.

Another reptile of note is the estuarine (saltwater) crocodile (*Crocodylus porosus*), which despite its common name inhabits freshwater habitats as well as salt. "Salties" can reach a length of 7m but specimens that large are unlikely here. They are mainly nocturnal and during the cooler months are often seen sunning themselves on mud and sand banks at low tide. See p42.

The Wet Tropics supports 53 frog species, of which 23 are rainforest dependent. All but two of the latter are endemics. One of the most beautiful is the orange-thighed tree frog (*Litoria xanthomera*), whose loud choruses can be heard after heavy spring and summer rain. It grows to a length of 65mm. Another impressive endemic, the northern barred frog (*Mixophyes shevilli*) reaches 110mm in length and is beautifully camouflaged for its life in the leaf litter.

Invertebrates

The diversity of invertebrate species in the rainforests of the Wet Tropics is simply mind-boggling. It's not known how many species occur here, but a survey carried out between the Russell River lowlands and the top of the Bellenden Ker Range identified 5000 of them. They included ants, bees, beetles, butterflies, centipedes, cicadas, flies, leeches, millipedes, mites, moths, scorpions, shrimps, snails, spiders, termites, ticks, wasps, worms and yabbies.

Apart from biting insects, the most obvious invertebrate is the gorgeous Ulysses butterfly (*Papilio ulysses*). It's often sighted flitting about on the forest margins and is readily identified from the electric-blue flash of its wings. The Wet Tropics is home to around 200 species of butterflies, most of which are seldom seen by the casual visitor. Largest of all is the birdwing butterfly (*Ornithoptera priamus*) with its wingspan of 200mm. The richly coloured male makes a spectacular sight as it swoops through the foliage.

Great Barrier Reef

The magical underwater wonderland that is the Great Barrier Reef covers 345,000 sq km and stretches for 2300km along the Queensland coast from Bundaberg to the tip of Cape York. This is the richest, most complex and diverse marine ecosystem on Earth, and it's said that an hour or two spent diving or snorkelling on it will turn you into a reef conservationist for life. The Reef was declared a marine park in 1975, and six years later it was added to UNESCO's World Heritage List.

It seems that coral reefs began to grow on Queensland's continental shelf around 18 million years ago as Australia drifted into clear tropical waters. Then followed a long period

17

during which the reefs waxed and waned as sea levels rose and fell. Today's Reef, which is built on a foundation of earlier reefs, dates from 8000 years ago when the last significant episode of rising sea level took place.

While the Reef is often thought of as being a single structure, it is in fact an intricate maze of around 2900 individual reefs ranging from solid platforms to complicated systems of lagoons and channels to long, narrow break-waters called "ribbon" reefs. The latter are found on the edge of the continental shelf and so form part of the 'real' Great Barrier Reef – the so-called Outer Reef. In FNQ the Outer Reef's distance from the coast varies from 32km off Cape Melville to around 60km off Cairns.

Also forming part of the Reef ecosystem are hundreds of continental islands and coral cays, extensive seagrass beds, and mangrove forests. Together these habitats support a staggering variety of marine life forms – around 1500 species of fish, at least 5000 molluscs, over 7500 crustaceans, 1500 sponges, and a similar diversity of other marine groups such as anemones and echinoderms.

As well, the Reef is home to around 30 species of marine mammals (dugongs, whales and dolphins) and numerous reptiles (marine turtles, crocodiles, eels and sea snakes). Huge breeding colonies of sea birds are found on some islands. Many species are found nowhere else, while for others, such as the endangered giant clam, dugong, green turtle and loggerhead turtle, the Reef is a stronghold of world significance.

The immense structures that make up the Great Barrier Reef are the work of tiny animals called polyps. Related to jellyfish, polyps have simple tube-like bodies with a ring of tentacles that surrounds a single opening (a combination mouth/anus) at the top.

Polyps live in a symbiotic relationship with algal cells called *zooxanthellae*. The latter convert sunlight into food, most of which is absorbed by the polyps. Indeed, it is the algal cells that supply most of the polyps' food. Meanwhile, the polyps secrete calcium

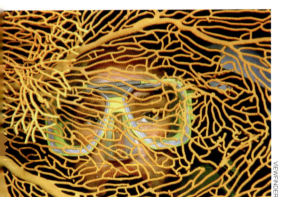

Gorgonian fan coral

Bannerfish

Giant soft coral tree

Daisy cup coral

carbonate, which provides them with a hard external skeleton. When polyps die, others build on top of their skeletons and so a reef is eventually formed. Live coral is just a thin veneer on top of a limestone substratum of dead animals, and it is the *zooxanthellae* that are responsible for its colouration.

The Reef's 360 species of hard corals produce growths in a spectacular variety of shapes, as indicated by their popular names – basket, brain, button, cup, daisy, fan, lettuce, mushroom, needle, plate, staghorn, table and so on. The reefs are at their most spectacular at night when the polyps, whose extended tentacles resemble exquisite flowers, are feeding.

Then there are the soft corals. Like their reef-building cousins, soft corals are made up of polyps, but they do not form limestone skeletons and can actually move around. They also come in an immense range of colours and forms, from tree-like growths to rubbery masses. The beautiful, filigreed gorgonian fans are among the most distinctive soft corals.

Juvenile spine cheeked anemone fish

Banded coral shrimp

Fish

When combined with the rich hues of corals and other life forms, the schools of brightly coloured reef fish form a shifting kaleidoscope that will hold you enthralled. The most beautiful tend to be the small and medium-sized species. Angel fish and butterfly fish are noted for the variety and brilliance of their markings; damsel fish form electric-blue schools that hover just above the corals; clown anemone fish wear striking white-and-orange stripes; parrotfish make up for their lack of elegance with gaudy colouration. The list goes on and on.

Reef fish also exhibit a huge variety of behaviours. Some are nocturnal, spending the daylight hours hiding from predators in caves and crevices. Some seek safety by gathering in large schools, while others are quite happy by themselves or in pairs. Cleaner wrasse (*Labroides dimidiatus*) remove parasites from the bodies, gills and mouths of other fish – they set up cleaning stations where customers wait for service. Juvenile blue spot (*Plectoropomus laevis*) defend themselves by mimicking the poisonous puffer fish. Butterfly fish (*Chaetodons*) and harlequin tusk fish (*Choerodon fasciatus*) establish territories and vigorously attack any hapless trespasser. Clown anemone fish (*Amphiprion percula*) lurk within the poisonous tentacles of reef anemones, luring other small fish into their deadly embrace and feeding on the scraps from the anemones' meals.

Crustaceans

There are a huge variety of crustaceans on the Reef. Most people are familiar with the sub-group known as decapods (shrimps, prawns, crabs and lobsters) as these are the ones that end up on dinner plates. Decapods are characterised by having external skeletons and five pairs of legs. The Reef has several species of large lobster (or crayfish) including the aptly named painted spiny lobster (*Panulirus versicolor*) with its brightly coloured patterns.

The crabs include hermit crabs that carry gastropod shells around with them in order to protect their soft abdomens – when the crab becomes too large for its shell it simply commandeers a new one to suit. When other crustaceans grow larger they must shed their external skeletons and grow replacements.

Threats to the Reef

There are several threats to the Great Barrier Reef's long-term survival, and the news that its coral cover has declined by half over the past 40 years is cause for grave concern – particularly as the most serious threats are either directly or indirectly attributable to human activities.

Global Warming

Global warming is by far the most important threat facing the Reef, and its effects are clearly visible as patches of hard coral that look as if they've been bleached. It appears that the relationship between the coral polyps and their *zooxanthellae* partners is finely tuned to work within a narrow band of water temperature. When this is exceeded the algal cells, instead of feeding the polyps, begin to poison them. To save themselves, the polyps must evict the cells. When they go, they take the colour with them – not to mention the polyps' major food source – and so the polyps' white skeletons are revealed. If the water temperatures return to normal quickly enough the *zooxanthellae* may recover, but if it takes too long the reef dies.

In 1998, a survey found that 42% of the Reef's coral cover was bleached to some extent and 18% was severely bleached. In 2002, these figures were 54% and 18% respectively. Some scientists believe that a one-degree increase in the average sea-surface temperature will raise the incidence of bleaching to 82%. A mere three-degree rise could literally wipe the coral out.

Crown-of-Thorns Starfish

Infestations of crown-of-thorns starfish are the next biggest threat, with about 10% of the Reef being severely affected by their depredations. This coral-eating species, which grows to a metre across, is native to northern Australian waters. A healthy reef can support up to 30 crown-of-thorns starfish per hectare, but occasionally something goes awry in the environment and triggers huge population explosions. It's not known why these outbreaks occur, but the most likely explanation is higher nutrient levels resulting from agricultural runoff. Overfishing may also play a part.

Other Threats

Other threats include long-term damage caused by cyclones, commercial fishing, deteriorating water quality, and tourism. There are 3700 professional fishers, including 550 trawler operators, operating within the marine park. Why a damaging activity like trawling should still be allowed on the Reef isn't quite clear.

Visitors can unwittingly damage coral by standing on it, touching it with their sunscreen lotion-covered fingers and knocking bits off with their snorkelling or dive gear. As there is potential for over a million tourists each year to do a lot of damage, the golden rules are:

- **Don't touch anything!**
- **Don't leave anything behind!**
- **Don't take anything away apart from memories and photographs!**

VIEWFINDER

Look but don't touch

Close-up of a giant clam

Bright pyramid butterfly fish and a school of fusiliers

Molluscs

Molluscs are a huge and varied group of marine creatures made up of gastropods, bivalves, nudibranchs and cephalopods. The Reef is home to over 4000 species of shell-producing molluscs alone.

Bivalves

Bivalves, which include oysters and clams, are characterised by having a skin flap called the mantle, which adds layer upon layer of calcium carbonate along the edge of the shell. The Reef's northern part is home to the world's largest bivalve, the giant clam (*Tridacna gigas*), which can grow to over a metre across and weigh 200kg.

Gastropods

Gastropods, or univalves, include slugs, snails and the cowries that are so popular with collectors. Other members of the group are the baler shells, which grow to 400mm in length and were used for baling water out of canoes. Cone shells (*Conus*) are another – these animals catch their prey by shooting out a barbed, venomous dart that has killed humans.

Cephalopods

Octopus, cuttlefish and squid seem unlikely molluscs, but they evolved from animals that had external skeletons. Cephalopods move with remarkable speed by taking water in and squirting it out – a form of jet propulsion. They are the chameleons of the marine world, changing colour at will in order to blend with their surroundings.

Nudibranchs

There are four main categories of nudibranchs, each having a respiratory organ exposed on its back. Nudibranchs come in an extraordinary variety of shapes and colours, but most are very small. One of the most spectacular is the Spanish dancer (*Hexabranchus sanguineus*), which, when disturbed, twists and turns about while swirling a vivid scarlet-orange 'cape'.

Echinoderms

The group of marine creatures known as echinoderms is made up of starfish (or sea stars), feather stars, brittle stars, sea cucumbers (or sea slugs) and sea urchins. While they can look very different to one another, all echinoderms share three characteristics – a symmetrical, five-part body plan; tube feet operated by hydraulic pressure; and a skeleton of calcite plates. The Reef has over 800 species of them.

Starfish

Starfish are brightly coloured, distinctively shaped creatures that are easily recognisable. Most have five arms – the infamous crown-of-thorns starfish (*Acanthaster planci*) has 15 – each of which has all the organs necessary for regeneration into a complete organism should the arm become detached. Some species – including the crown-of-thorns – feed by turning their stomach out through their mouth and spreading it over the food, which is consumed externally. One of the most conspicuous starfishes is the blue sea star (*Linckia laevigata*) with its vivid colouration.

Feather Stars

Named for their feathery appearance (the result of numerous side structures called pinnules), feather stars can move around and even swim, but spend most of their time anchored in a good feeding position. Their ancestors dominated the seas 300 million years ago, making feather stars the most primitive echinoderms.

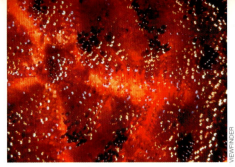

Close-up of a fire urchin

Brittle Stars

Brittle stars are named for their habit of dropping their segmented arms when threatened. These creatures are the fastest moving echinoderms thanks to their long arms, which 'sweep' them along. Some species have extra-long, smooth arms and these are called serpent stars. While brittle stars are common they tend to be nocturnal and so are not often seen.

Sea Urchins

Sea urchins have a solid skeleton covered in sharp and sometimes poisonous spines, and some species also have strong defensive pincers (as do some starfish). Yet despite this formidable protection, parrotfish and crabs can still prey upon them. Many sea urchins hide during the day when their enemies are most active.

Sea Cucumbers

Sea cucumbers, or bêches-de-mer, breathe through their skin and feeding tentacles, and, in some cases, their anus which is also commonly the home of pearl fish and small crabs. In some species the anus has evolved into a means of defence – it ejects sticky tubules that cause intruders to become entangled. Other species literally disintegrate when threatened but can reconstitute themselves when the danger is past. ■

Dugongs in Trouble

Growing to 3m long and weighing up to 400kg, the dugong (*Dugong dugon*) is our only marine mammal herbivore. The dugong and its North American counterpart, the manatee, form the order of *Sirenia* (sea cows), which are related to elephants. Instead of hind limbs, dugongs have a horizontally flattened tail, while the forelimbs are modified as paddles.

The dugong is found in warm, shallow coastal waters of the Indian and western Pacific oceans, where it spends most of its time grazing on seagrasses. In Australia, which has most of the world's population of dugong, it occurs right around the north coast from Shark Bay to Moreton Bay.

Australia has around 80,000 dugongs, with 12,000 of these living on the Great Barrier Reef mostly north of Cooktown. The most important area for dugong in FNQ is the Hinchinbrook Channel, which has extensive seagrass meadows. There is comparatively little seagrass between here and Cooktown, so dugongs only occur in low densities in that area.

Dugongs are classified as vulnerable to extinction throughout their range. They are fast vanishing from the Great Barrier Reef south of Cooktown, where their numbers declined by 50% between 1986 and 1994. Because they reproduce only slowly, the loss of more than one or two per cent of adult females to unnatural causes can be disastrous.

The major threats to dugongs are all related to human activity. One is the damage caused to seagrass meadows by the dumping of dredge spoil, the heavy discharge of sediments from rivers, and trawling. A severely affected meadow may take a decade to recover.

Another threat is boat strikes. Not only are dugongs injured and killed by collisions with boats and propellers, an increase in traffic can frighten them away from the area. Hunting, fishing nets and shark nets also kill an unknown number of these inoffensive creatures.

Information Sources

Tourist Offices

The main visitor information office for Far North Queensland is the Gateway Discovery Centre in Cairns, 51 The Esplanade, ℂ 07 4051 3588, www.tropicalaustralia.com. It opens daily from 8.30am to 5.30pm (public holidays 10am to 2pm).

Elsewhere there are good information centres in Atherton, Cardwell, Cooktown, Herberton, Innisfail, Kuranda, Malanda, Mission Beach, Port Douglas, Ravenshoe and Tully. See the sections on these places for contact details.

Government Offices

All national parks (including islands on the Great Barrier Reef), conservation parks and state forests are managed by the **Queensland Parks & Wildlife Service** (QPWS, www.epa.qld.gov.au). The Cairns regional office and information centre is at 5B Sheridan St, ℂ 07 4046 6600, in the city centre. Any inquiries regarding activities such as bushwalking, mountain biking and canoeing in national parks or state forests should be directed here in the first instance. If the office staff can't answer your questions they'll direct you to someone who can.

Information on the Great Barrier Reef Marine Park is available from the **Great Barrier Reef Marine Park Authority** (GBRMPA, ℂ 1800 990 177, www.gbrmpa.gov.au) in Townsville. Its contact point in Cairns is the QPWS office.

The **Wet Tropics Management Authority** (ℂ 07 4052 0555, www.wettropics.gov.au) is at 15 Lake St, Cairns. It looks after the World Heritage values of the Wet Tropics WHA and has information on public-use areas that fall outside the national parks and state forests (e.g. the CREB Track). Visitors will find most of its publications at the QPWS office.

Other Useful Sources

Motoring

The Cairns office of the Royal Automobile Club of Queensland (RACQ, ℂ 07 4033 6433, www.racq.com.au) is at 537 Mulgrave Rd, in Earlville. The bookshop on the premises sells touring maps and other publications.

Do your homework before venturing off the beaten track, in this case out to the Palmer River goldfield at Maytown

ROB VAN DRIESUM

Planning the Trip

Eco-Tourism

A lot of tourist operators use the 'e' word, but not all of them comply with the official definition of eco-tourism as laid down by Eco-Tourism Australia (ETA), the peak national body for the eco-tourism industry – "Eco-tourism is ecologically sustainable tourism with a primary focus on experiencing natural areas that fosters environmental and cultural understanding, appreciation and conservation."

Check the ETA's website, www.ecotourism.org.aus, to find out if a particular 'eco-business' is properly accredited.

Books & Magazines

A number of guidebooks deal with specific activities such as fishing and these are listed elsewhere in this book. However, useful references of a general nature are in such short supply that we could only find one – Lonely Planet's *Queensland* (2002). It includes quite a bit of information on the Cairns region. A new edition incorporating Lonely Planet's separate book to the islands of the Barrier Reef is due out in August 2005.

Exploring Queensland's Parks & Forests (2003, Environmental Protection Agency) is a glovebox-sized reference that contains brief details of most national parks, conservation parks and state forests in FNQ.

Tropical Topics – A Second Compilation (2000, Reef Research Centre) is a collection of informative newsletters that cover various aspects of the Great Barrier Reef's ecosystem. It's available at the QPWS office in Cairns.

Maps

The maps in the back of this book come from Hema's *Townsville-Cairns-Cooktown* map, at a scale of 1:600,000. Other good touring maps giving partial coverage of the Cairns region include Hema's *Cairns to Cooktown* (1:250,000) and *Atherton Tableland* (1:250,000); and Sunmap's *Cairns & Region* (1:100,000).

Also by Hema, the *Cairns & Region Street Directory* will get you around the Cairns metropolitan area and several other regional centres. If you're only in town for a few days, Hema's *Cairns & Region* (1:22,500) may suffice.

More detail is provided on the topographic sheets published by Geoscience (formerly AUSLIG). In Cairns these are available from Absell's Chart & Map Centre (℡ 07 4051 2699) in the Andrejic Arcade at 55-59 Lake St; and the Department of Natural Resources & Mines (℡ 07 4039 8431) at 5B Sheridan St.

When to Go

Depending on what you want to do, any time can be a good time to be in FNQ. For birdwatchers the most fruitful time to be there is mid-spring to early summer – say, October to January. The waterfalls are at their most spectacular during the Wet from January onwards, when all that rain brings dramatic renewal to the land – this period is best for white-water kayaking and river and estuary fishing. However, the height of the Wet is not an ideal time for bush camping or rainforest walks on unmade paths, while four-wheel-driving is pretty much out of the question then.

Climate

The Cairns region has a monsoonal climate with distinct wet and dry seasons. Thunderstorms herald the approach of the Wet in November and the rains have usually set in with a vengeance by early January. April brings the end of the rainy season and the beginning of the long Dry – which on occasion can also be quite wet. Cairns receives a respectable average annual rainfall of 1995mm, whereas Babinda (Australia's wettest town) is inundated by a whopping 4200mm. Further south, Tully holds the record for Australia's highest

Fierce thunderstorms herald the build-up to the Wet

annual rainfall ever in a town (7900mm), while the wettest place on the Australian mainland is the top of the Bellenden Ker Range, which receives an average of 7800mm. To the west, Chillagoe is much drier, receiving an annual average of 683mm.

The southeast trade winds blow steadily for days and weeks on end during the dry season, stirring up the water close to shore and restricting small craft to sheltered waters. September brings calmer conditions as winds swing around to the northeast. November to March is the cyclone season, with an average of two cyclones occurring off the coast each year. Radio stations broadcast ample warnings whenever a cyclone threatens, giving you plenty of time to get out of the way.

In Cairns, average minimum/maximum temperatures range from 23.6/31.4°C in January to 17.1/25.6°C in July. Meanwhile, up on the Atherton Tableland, temperatures are usually several degrees cooler than on the coast. Frosts are not uncommon here, so don't forget the winter woollies. Cool winter nights are the norm in the region's western parts.

Crowds

May to October brings pleasantly warm, dry conditions that lure southerners en masse for a winter holiday in the tropics. The main crowd danger period coincides with the winter months, and conditions are extreme during the July and September school breaks. It would be wise to make key bookings for accommodation and tours well in advance during these periods.

Rush hour on the Green Island jetty. Book key accommodation and tours in advance during busy periods

National Park Permits

Entry to all national parks in FNQ is free. A nominal fee is charged for camping (see Where to Stay, below), and a "permit to traverse" is required before you can drive a car or ride a mountain bike on many state forest roads. Application forms are available at QPWS offices and major visitor information centres – allow two working days for your application to be processed, though during quiet periods you may receive your permit on the spot. The purpose of the exercise is to regulate visitor numbers and ensure that routes don't become too crowded.

Special Precautions

When you list them, FNQ seems to have more than its fair share of annoying or dangerous flora and fauna. Fortunately a few simple precautions will help you avoid falling foul of most of them.

The worst hazards of all are **estuarine (saltwater) crocodiles**, **marine stingers** and **venomous snakes**, as an encounter with any of them will have painful and possibly fatal consequences – for you. In the case of the first two, just stay out of their habitat and you'll be fine (see the boxed texts on p42 and p50). With snakes, be observant when you're on a bushwalk and wear long trousers and boots. Make enough noise and they'll usually slither away before you get too close. Also be aware of how to deal with snakebite.

Blood-sucking insects such as **mosquitoes**, **march flies** and **sand flies** (also known as midges) can be particularly troublesome in some places, such as in or near mangrove forests. In fact, they may literally ruin your day if you've failed to pack the repellent (*Rid* is a popular brand) and aren't wearing sensible clothing (i.e. light-coloured, loose-fitting, and with maximum skin coverage). If you're camping or caravanning, make sure all insect screening is finely meshed and in excellent condition before leaving home. March flies and sand flies are inactive at night.

Cairns's UV index can be quite high despite the apparent mildness of its maximum temperatures. Sensible visitors avoid **sunburn** by practising the "slip, slop, slap" routine. Those who simply must take a tan home with them should do their sunbaking before 10am and after 3pm, when UV levels are less hazardous.

Rainforest Safety

Be aware of the following pests when bush-walking in forested areas:

Scrub mites are best avoided by sitting on a groundsheet rather than on the forest floor or dead logs. An intense itching sensation in the sweaty parts is a good indication that mites have set up residence.

Ticks are usually brushed onto your body when you walk through tall grass or dense undergrowth. Wear long trousers stuffed into your socks and a long-sleeved shirt, and spray repellent onto your clothing. Check your body thoroughly after bushwalking in forested areas and, if you find a tick, dab insecticide on it before removing it. Some people suffer an allergic reaction to tick bites, and this can be serious. Seek medical advice if headache, nausea, paralysis or unusual rashes develop.

Leeches can be a nuisance in wet areas, but the liberal application of repellent to your socks at ankle height usually keeps them at bay (tea-tree oil seems to work well). If a leech manages to breach the defences, simply apply roll-on repellent or salt to its bloated backside and it'll drop off. The bite will bleed for a while and may itch for days, but is usually harmless if you sterilise it and cover it up to prevent further infection.

A couple of plants to avoid are **lawyer vines**, also known as wait-a-while – an attractive climbing palm whose hooked tendrils can become entangled in your clothing as you brush past them – and **stinging plants**. The latter prefer disturbed areas of the rainforest (e.g. along roads and walking tracks) and have large, heart-shaped leaves covered with fine hairs. These break off in your skin, where they release an irritant poison causing sometimes excruciating pain that can persist for days if not weeks. There's no known cure (though waxing may alleviate the worst pain), and the best strategy is to avoid touching any plant with heart-shaped leaves until you learn which one to watch out for – hopefully this knowledge won't come through bitter experience.

Security

Last but by no means least of local hazards are the **thieves** that hang around parking areas for the purpose of breaking into parked vehicles – a practice by no means confined to FNQ. Leaving valuables in full view on the seat is simply begging to be robbed. The best precaution is to carry your camera, holiday funds, credit cards, medical prescriptions etc with you at all times and lock any other valuable items in the car boot. Keep in mind that it only takes these thieving bastards a few seconds to break into the average car and clean it out.

Where to Stay

You'll find plenty of accommodation of all kinds in and around Cairns and the coastal resort towns of Mission Beach and Port Douglas, where luxury resorts and holiday apartments have proliferated in recent years. Budget accommodation in particular is at a

No shortage of advice and regulations at Garners Beach, near Mission Beach

The fine hairs of the notorious stinging tree, with its distinctive, heart-shaped leaves, can cause excruciating pain that lasts for weeks. Take care!

premium during busy times, when an army of holiday-makers and grey nomads fills caravan parks and campgrounds.

The RACQ publishes annual accommodation and caravan park directories. These are free to members of interstate motoring organisations.

For something a little different, why not spend a night or three indulging yourself as the guest of an island resort? There are several such places scattered along the coast and staying there won't necessarily gobble up your life savings. The beauty of it is that once the day-trippers have departed, the island belongs to you and a handful of fellow guests. Who needs to camp to get away from it all?

A number of rainforest accommodation places are owned by wildlife enthusiasts who've made bird and mammal viewing a speciality of the house. An example is Chambers Wildlife Rainforest Lodge (℗ 07 4095 3754) near Lake Eacham, where you can observe a host of birds such as eastern whipbirds, spotted catbirds and Victoria's riflebirds by day, and red-legged pademelons and sugar gliders by night. Check with local visitor information centres for more.

Houseboats

For something entirely different you can hire a houseboat and cruise the sheltered waters of Lake Tinaroo and the Hinchinbrook Channel. However, options are limited, so don't leave it too late to book:

Many QPWS camping areas must be booked in advance. Plan ahead to avoid disappointment

- **Hinchinbrook Rent-a-Yacht** – based at Cardwell with a range of houseboats for hire. Activities are restricted to the Hinchinbrook Channel and the Gould Island/Mission Bay area at the northern end of Hinchinbrook Island (℗ 07 4066 8007, www.hinchinbrookrentayacht.com.au).
- **Tinaroo Tropical Houseboats** – based at Kairi near Lake Tinaroo with two to six-berth craft (℗ 07 4095 8322, www.lake tinaroo.com).

Camping in National Parks

Many national parks and state forests have camping areas managed by the QPWS. Some of these are relatively sophisticated, with defined sites, barbecues, picnic facilities, toilets and cold-water showers. Others are little more than clearings in the forest. While some are suitable for caravans, powered sites are nonexistent.

Although it covers the whole state, *Camping Queensland* (2004, Environmental Protection Agency) is an essential reference. It includes general information and details of all camping areas – including privately owned ones – in national parks and state forests in the Cairns region.

Rules & Regulations

The usual common-sense rules and regulations apply:

- **Campfires** are banned except in fireplaces where these are provided. Firewood is supplied in some places, otherwise you'll have to bring your own – or use a gas stove. Use supplied firewood sparingly, and make sure the fire is out before you break camp.
- **Toilets** are provided in the more popular places. Where they aren't, bury human waste at least 50m from any stream, lake or walking track.
- **Rubbish** should be disposed of either in bins (where provided) or at approved collection points.
- **Pets** are not permitted.
- **Camp** only in defined sites or existing cleared areas.
- **Generators** are banned from most places – observe advisory signage.
- **Feeding** the wildlife is prohibited – the practice is harmful for the animals and also encourages aggressive behaviour towards campers.

- **Polluting** streams or lakes with soap, shampoo and detergents is prohibited.
- **Noxious** weeds can easily be spread from place to place – check your camping gear before leaving home and when breaking camp, and dispose of any suspicious seeds.
- **Limits** apply to lengths of stay.
- **Water**, where provided, should be boiled before drinking.

A few additional rules apply on islands in the Great Barrier Reef Marine Park:

- **Coral reefs** are easily damaged. Do not attempt to cross fringing reefs when there is insufficient water to get your craft across without dragging it – wait for the right tide.
- **Anchor** in sand or mud rather than on coral – use a lightweight reef pick with plastic tubing over the anchor chain. Park your kayak above the high-tide mark.
- **Cyclones** and storms are risky on small islands – evacuate immediately if the weather looks like turning bad. Always carry extra food and water in case you get stuck.
- **Restrictions** or bans may be in force on activities such as line fishing and the collecting of seashells – check the GBRMPA zoning plan for your area.

QPWS Fees & Bookings

The use of QPWS-managed campsites in national parks and forests is subject to a permit, which costs $4/16 per person/family per night.

Some camping areas have a self-registration system whereby intending campers, on arrival at the campground, complete a form and deposit the fee or credit-card details in the box provided. For others you *must* book a site in advance – online at www.qld.gov.au/camping or by phoning ℂ131304 on weekdays 8am-6pm,

Saturdays 8am-4.45pm. In this book we've mentioned the pre-booking requirement for a few of the more popular sites, but the situation is fluid and we cannot guarantee which of the two systems will apply at your chosen site. Obviously it's wise to check ahead to avoid disappointment.

Privately owned areas, such as the Lava Lodge camping area at the edge of the Undara Volcanic National Park, have their own fees and payment systems.

Getting Around

Self-drivers will find it easy to get around the Cairns region, although visitors from flat places may find that the steeper, more tortuous roads take a bit of getting used to. Most of the major land-based tourist attractions are connected to Cairns by mostly good bitumen roads. Dirt roads are mainly confined to state forest areas and national parks, and around more remote towns such as Chillagoe, Cooktown and Laura.

Minor roads through state forests tend to be narrow and winding, with many blind corners posing the ever-present risk of a collision with oncoming traffic. Good examples include the Daintree-Cape Tribulation road, the Ravenshoe-Tully Falls road, and the Danbulla Forest Drive. Drive carefully!

Wildlife is an ever-present hazard in forest areas. Cassowaries are large birds, and they don't look both ways before stepping onto the road. Speed limits in cassowary strongholds tend to be far too high – even 50km/h can be an unsafe speed in such areas.

Roads throughout the region are subject to closure during the wet season. Check the RACQ's statewide road condition report on ℂ1300130595.

Caravans

Many of the region's minor roads are not recommended for caravans, the common limiting factors being road width, frontal visibility and traction. Examples include the Kennedy-Blencoe Falls road; the Bloomfield Track between Cape Tribulation and the Bloomfield River; the Danbulla Forest Drive; the Old Palmerston Hwy; and the Millaa Millaa Waterfall Circuit. You also have to be game to take a large caravan on the narrow, winding road from the Daintree River crossing to Cape Tribulation, but some do it! ∎

Drive carefully in cassowary habitat (here near Cape Trib)

Chapter Three

What to Do

Land-Based Activities

Bushwalking

Bushwalking is a popular activity and there are numerous established routes. These vary from sealed pathways to goat tracks that lead you over tangled tree roots on steep, slippery slopes. Minor forestry roads are another option in many areas.

You'll find dozens of short walks (i.e. less than 40 minutes return), and these are generally fine for families – some are wheelchair-friendly. This category generally provides access to specific points of interest such as waterfalls, special trees and lookouts. Many are interpretive walks with signs that give information topics such as flora and fauna, natural history and Aboriginal traditions. The Daintree-Cape Tribulation area has several excellent interpretive boardwalks that explain the rainforest's evolution.

Some of the longer routes are well made, but others, such as the Mt Bartle Frere track, are largely unimproved and can be extremely strenuous. These are definitely not suitable for the inexperienced walker. As well, the more remote tracks are often poorly marked, and those who don't remain alert can easily lose their way.

Wooroonooran has a number of options including challenging treks over the Bellenden Ker Range and short walks to scenic highlights like Josephine Falls. Barron Gorge National Park near Cairns also has a good selection, and you can even go bushwalking near the city centre. In the south, between Ravenshoe and Tully, the Misty Mountains feature a network of high-altitude rainforest walks.

Other routes of note include the Thorsborne Track on Hinchinbrook Island; the Bump Track near Port Douglas; the circuit walk around Lake Barrine on the Atherton Tableland; the Lacey Creek-Licuala link track near Mission Beach; and the Edmund Kennedy Memorial Walking Track, also near Mission Beach. The region's longest walking route is Section One of the Bicentennial National Trail, which wends its way southwards for 470km along the Great Dividing Range from Cooktown to near Mount Garnet.

Safe Walking

The most comfortable time to go bushwalking is April to October. Unmade tracks become far too soggy and slippery during the Wet, when you're better off sticking to sealed paths and boardwalks. This being the tropics, walkers who aren't acclimatised will perspire freely when exerting themselves – just thinking about physical activity can bring you out in a lather of sweat! Avoid dehydration by drinking plenty of water, not soft drinks or diuretics like coffee and alcohol. To be on the safe side, boil creek water before drinking it.

Time out while hiking near Babinda

TOURISM QUEENSLAND

29

Be aware too that weather conditions can change dramatically and unexpectedly at the higher altitudes, such as on top of the Bellenden Ker Range. A calm, sunny day can quickly degenerate, making hypothermia a real danger. Always carry warm clothing, wet-weather gear and emergency rations when venturing into these areas.

If you intend to do any overnight treks that involve camping in the rainforest, take precautions against the dreaded white-tailed rat. These camp-robbing, rabbit-sized rodents aren't dangerous, but they can make a damned nuisance of themselves by chewing their way into rucksacks and even metal boxes in search of food. They are great climbers, so there's no point hanging your pack in a tree unless it's suspended on a length of wire. Apparently even that isn't totally effective.

See Special Precautions on p25-26 for other hazards such as stinging plants and blood-sucking invertebrates.

Finally, always advise a responsible friend of your plans before setting out on long or remote walks. Arrange a time for the authorities to be alerted if you don't call in by the appointed time. It goes without saying – but we'll say it anyway – that you must make a point of contacting your friend immediately on finishing the walk.

If serious hiking is not for you, there are many excellent short walks, such as here amid the fan palms in Licuala State Forest near Mission Beach

Information

There is at least rudimentary information available for most public walking tracks, and you can usually pick up leaflets from QPWS offices and visitor information centres. Always check with rangers for up-to-date track conditions and other advice before attempting the more remote walks.

There are several guidebooks devoted to walking and trekking in FNQ. Paul Curtis's *The Travellers' Guide to North Queensland (Cairns & Surrounds)* covers 52 suggested weekend trips between Ingham and Cooktown and west to Undara. Kym Dungey & Jane Whytlaw have put together a series of five excellent booklets under the *Tropical Walking Tracks* banner. Each one covers a particular area – Townsville to Tully; The Cassowary Coast; Cairns & Kuranda; Atherton Tableland; and Port Douglas, the Daintree & Cooktown.

The Wet Tropics Management Authority website, www.wettropics.gov.au, has details of many walks. Check the Tablelands Walking Club website (see below) for some practical advice.

Bushwalking Clubs

There are two bushwalking clubs in the region and both welcome experienced walkers on their excursions. These clubs are excellent sources of information on local conditions:

- **Cairns Bushwalking Club** – PO Box 1397, Cairns 4870, ✆ 07 4054 2028 or 4055 3445, cairnsbushwalkers@iig.com.au
- **Tablelands Walking Club** – PO Box 642, Herberton 4872, http://users.qldnet.com.au/~tablelandwalk, or try Col Wilson on ✆ 07 4092 3249

Organised Tours

Commercial operators are thin on the ground:

- **Bike N Hike** – Port Douglas; half-day and day walks incorporating the Bump Track and Big Mowbray Falls (✆ 07 4099 4000, www.bikenhike.com.au)
- **Wilderness Expeditions** – Herberton; day walks in the hills around Herberton as well as overnight and extended treks with pack donkeys (✆ 07 4096 2266, www.wildex.com.au)
- **Wooroonooran Safaris** – day walk over the Goldfield Trail in Wooroonooran National Park (✆ 07 4051 5512, www.wooroonooran-safaris.com.au)

Beach Walking

Far North Queensland has an abundance of fine beaches, and some provide a true wilderness experience where the only footprints you'll see will probably be your own. Examples include Edmund Kennedy National Park near Cardwell; Ella Beach and Bramston Beach near Innisfail; Back Beach near Yarrabah; Emmagen Beach near Cape Tribulation; and Cedar Bay near Cooktown.

There are a couple of safety issues other than protecting yourself against sunburn and biting insects. First is the danger posed by lurking saltwater crocodiles, which inhabit estuarine waters along the coast. As a rule of thumb, if you find your way blocked by a flooded estuary, turn around and head homewards. *Don't* try to swim across it.

Second is the requirement to plan walks around the tides so that you won't become trapped by rising waters – it's best to start your walk on a receding tide. Tide times between Cardwell and Cooktown are listed inside the back page of *The Cairns Post*.

Mountain Biking

Another great way to experience the forests of FNQ is by mountain bike, but you need to be fit to tackle the many steep ascents. There are just as many steep down slopes, too – in fact, this region has some of Australia's best downhill riding.

Most of the better known venues are shared by motor vehicles, although traffic is generally light – particularly where a QPWS "permit to traverse" is required. Worthwhile shorter options include the 48km Black Mountain Rd between Kuranda and Julatten (p73); the Tinaroo Range Network near Mareeba; and the 26km Bump Track near Port Douglas (p32).

An interesting day outing near Cairns combines the Black Mountain Rd (starting at the Kuranda end) with the Bump Track, then continues on to Port Douglas where you catch Quicksilver's fast catamaran back to Cairns. Another good day trip is a cycle through the Misty Mountains from Ravenshoe to the Palmerston Hwy via Maalan Rd, Sutties Gap Rd, Maple Creek Rd and K-Tree Rd. The best approach here is to stay overnight in Ravenshoe and get an early start.

For an enjoyable two-day ride, consider the

Bramston Beach near Innisfail, ideal for solitary walks

Mount Garnet-Blencoe Falls-Kennedy track, with an overnight camp at Blencoe Falls en route. Start at Mount Garnet for the easiest ride as the trend is downhill. A worthwhile longer ride is Section One (Cooktown to Gunnawarra) of the Bicentennial National Trail (p39). If you're tackling the CREB Track (p37), start at the Cooktown end as the slopes are less savage from that direction.

One unique hazard to be aware of is the dreaded lawyer vine. The hooked tendrils of this climbing palm are often seen hanging over little-used rainforest roads and tracks. A slap across the face or bare arm from one of these things is a most unpleasant and painful experience, as is unhooking yourself afterwards. Keep your eyes peeled.

Riders should wear a helmet (a mandatory requirement on public roads) and brightly coloured clothing, and carry plenty of drinking water. Beware of oncoming traffic on narrow forest roads.

Information

The easiest way to find out about mountain-bike routes in specific state forests is to ring the Cairns QPWS office. Alternatively, experienced local rider Struan Lamont (☎ 07 4034 2768) is happy to give advice and point visitors in the right direction. You can also check the Cairns Mountain Bike Club's website, www.cairnsmtb.com.

Don't forget that you may need a QPWS permit to cycle on minor roads and walking tracks within state forest areas.

ROB VAN DRIESUM

While cycling (or walking, for that matter), beware of the hooked tendrils of the lawyer vine, also known as wait-a-while for obvious reasons!

The Bump Track

(p113, D6)

Discovered by the bushman Christie Palmerston in 1877, the wagon road over the Great Dividing Range from Port Douglas to the Hodgkinson River Goldfield was a vital transport link for the mines and cattle stations then being established in the hinterland. Known as the Bump Track, this rugged jungle trail was so steep that it took a team of 66 straining bullocks to haul one 13-tonne boiler from the port to the top of the range. No doubt the bullockies shouted themselves hoarse, but fortunately there were a number of wayside hotels where they could lubricate their throats.

Today the first 26km of the Bump Track is preserved as a multi-use route for walking, mountain biking and horse riding. En route there are impressive views of the ranges and Big Mowbray Falls, and plenty of beautiful World Heritage rainforest. Mountain bikers and horse riders require a QPWS "permit to traverse" to use the track.

The Bump Track can be accessed off the Black Mountain Rd at its western end (see the boxed text p73) and Port Douglas in the east. To get there from Port Douglas, take the Captain Cook Hwy south from Craiglie for 1.5km, then turn right into Mowbray River Rd and onto Connolly Rd for 3.5km.

See the different Organised Tours sections elsewhere on these pages for organised walking, mountain-biking and horse-riding tours along the Bump Track.

Organised Tours

There are a couple of commercial operators and both offer a variety of rides including charters. Both also provide a pick-up/drop-off service, which can come in handy on a one-way trip. A discount generally applies if you use your own bike.

- **Bike N Hike** – several half and full-day rainforest rides near Port Douglas, including the Bump Track, as well as charters on the Black Mountain Rd and the CREB Track with an option to continue on to Cooktown (☎ 07 4099 4000, www.bikenhike.com.au)
- **Dan's Mountain Biking** – a variety of half-day, full day and night rides on forest tracks between Cairns and Cape Tribulation, and charters to places like the CREB Track and the Misty Mountains (☎ 07 4032 0066, www.cairns.aust.com/mtb)

Watching Wildlife

Birds

With some 430 species of birds found in the Wet Tropics and Great Barrier Reef areas, FNQ has a lot to offer the visiting birder. The number of ornithological tours and guiding services confirms this.

The best time to visit Cairns on a birding holiday is October to January. Many rainforest trees are fruiting then; water-bird populations have become concentrated around the permanent wetlands; migrants are here to escape winter; and Australian migrants, having wintered in places like New Guinea, have returned home to breed.

There are countless good places to see native bird life. Lowland and upland rainforests are generally rich in species and between them contain the Wet Tropics' 12 endemics (see Birds on pp15-16). The ribbons of rainforest that follow streams through dry sclerophyll forest are usually good places to try, while mangrove forests have their own suite of species.

While not exactly Cairns's scenic highlight, the mud flats along the Esplanade are great for bird-watchers. To the chagrin of those who would like to see the mud disappear under tourism developments, this visually unprepossessing area is recognised internationally as being a major shorebird habitat. Over 200 species of all kinds have been recorded here, including many migrants.

Michaelmas Cay near Cairns is a major breeding ground for sea birds, particularly terns and noddies. It can be visited on a tour from Palm Cove. Tens of thousands of pied imperial pigeons (also known as Torres Strait pigeons) migrate from New Guinea each year in September to nest on the Brook Islands, off the northern end of Hinchinbrook Island. Sadly, visits during the breeding season are severely restricted.

Eubenangee Swamp near Innisfail and Hasties Swamp near Atherton are major waterbird habitats. A bird hide makes things easy at the latter, but you'll need a good telescope at Eubenangee, as the viewing point is some distance from the action. Saltwater crocodiles can often be seen here as well.

As you'd expect, anywhere close to a diversity of major habitats is likely to present good birding. The Daintree River is one, with many local species being best seen from the river. Mount Molloy is another. In fact, Mount Molloy is central to one of Australia's richest birding areas, with nearly 300 species (including all the endemics) recorded within a 15km radius of town. Sightings of over 180 species have been recorded from both the Mareeba Tropical Savannah & Wetland Reserve and the Crater Lakes National Park, on the Atherton Tableland.

Information

Lloyd Neilsen's excellent *Birds of Queensland's Wet Tropics & Great Barrier Reef* is an essential reference for keen birders. Small enough for the glove box and day pack, it contains a wealth of information including bird identification, habitats and birding hot spots.

Other Wildlife

While birds attract most of the attention overall, there are some popular targets in the reptilian and mammalian worlds. One sought-after reptile is the saltwater crocodile, and the Daintree River is the major hot spot for these prehistoric beasts. The best chance of finding them (short of going for a swim) is to take a river cruise at low tide in the cooler months, when they can be seen basking on mud banks. Check tide times in *The Cairns Post* before you book. As the weather warms up, progressively less adult salties are seen until by December the river seems to have been taken over by juveniles. It hasn't!

Other interesting reptiles include forest dragons and amethystine pythons, which the quiet observer may see sunning themselves on the rainforest margins. Good places to spot them are Lake Tinaroo, Lake Eacham and Lake Barrine, all on the Atherton Tableland.

The musky rat kangaroo is a diurnal species that is often seen foraging on the forest floor. Agile wallabies are a common sight in open forest and grasslands near streams in the early morning and late afternoon.

These are also the best times to see platypuses, which are common in eastward flowing streams south of Cooktown. Some places, such as Yungaburra and Atherton, have purpose-built platypus observation platforms and these are good starting points. You'll need to be very quiet as platypuses are shy animals with acute hearing.

Spotlighting in the rainforests can reveal nocturnal animals such as brown tree snakes, frogs, owls, native rodents, bats, bandicoots, possums and tree kangaroos. High-altitude rainforest areas such as Mt Hypipamee National Park near Atherton are good places to see endemic possum and tree kangaroos.

The Cairns mudflats are a good spot to observe water birds

DENIS O'BYRNE

To spotlight successfully you will obviously need a powerful torch – a maximum of 30 watts is recommended for wildlife within 20m. Hold the torch in front of you at about eye level and look along the beam while slowly moving it over the ground or vegetation. When you see an eye-shine (the torchlight reflecting off an animal's eyes) hold the light steady until you've identified the animal, then attach a red cellophane filter for the purpose of viewing it.

Organised Tours & Guiding Services

A number of tour operators, particularly in the Daintree, offer river cruises and guided day and night interpretive walks that introduce you to the region's flora and fauna. The more specialised ones include:

- **Alan's Wildlife Tours** – Alan Gillanders offers early morning, half and full-day bird-watching tours on the Atherton Tableland. His 1.5hr nocturnal tour departs from Yungaburra on the Atherton Tableland (℡ 07 4095 3784, spotlighting@cyberwizards.com.au).

- **Australian Natural History Tours** – David Armbrust runs half and full-day wildlife tours in rainforest and eucalypt forest west of Port Douglas (℡ 07 4094 1600, www.anhs.com.au).

- **Australian Wildlife Tours** – has a couple of evening rainforest spotlighting tours and also offers charter and specialised trips (℡ 07 4093 7287, www.australiawildlifetours.com).

- **Chris Dahlberg's Specialised River Tours** – Chris operates on the Daintree River and specialises in birds. Around 50 species, including the great-billed heron, can usually be seen on his two-hour dawn cruise (℡ 07 4098 7997, htpp://home.austarnet.com.au/chrisld).

- **Dan Irby's Mangrove Adventures** – informative natural history tours with a wildlife bias on the Daintree River (℡ 07 4090 7017, www.mangroveadven.citysearch.com.au).

- **Fine Feather Tours** – operating in the Mossman area, naturalist Del Richards has a full-day bird safari that features seven habitats and, on average, more than 90 species. Over 55 species are usually seen on his morning wildlife safari (℡ 07 4094 1199, www.finefeathertours.com.au).

- **Wait-a-While Rainforest Tours** – night and day wildlife-watching trips to the Atherton Tableland and the Daintree (℡ 07 4098 2422, www.waitawhile.com.au)

- **Wildscapes Safaris** – offers a morning platypus and bird-watching tour and an evening tour spotlighting nocturnal animals (℡ 07 4057 6272, www.wildscapes-safaris.com.au).

- **Wild Watch** – Jonathon Munro leads guided wildlife excursions of a few hours to seven days or longer in the Cairns, Daintree, Misty Mountains and Atherton Tableland areas (℡ 07 4093 9803, www.wildwatch.com.au).

Eastern water dragon

Agile wallabies are a common sight in the early morning or late afternoon

Gold & Gem Fossicking

Far North Queensland has two designated gemstone fossicking areas. There are also a few gold and tin mining areas – such as the Palmer River and Hodgkinson River goldfields – where you can fossick provided you have the landholder's written permission.

The designated fossicking areas are off Hwy 1 at Mt Gibson (near Innot Hot Springs) and O'Briens Creek (near Mount Surprise). Here, alluvial and colluvial deposits yield gem-quality topaz, most of it colourless. Water is generally scarce, so the main recovery method is dry sieving – 6mm and 9mm mesh is recommended.

Camping is not permitted at either of these places. However, Innot Hot Springs, which has a caravan park, is only 5km from Mt Gibson, and there's a basic camping area 4km from O'Briens Creek on the road from Mount Surprise. During the dry season both areas are normally accessible to conventional vehicles driven with care.

Information & Permits

Anyone fossicking for minerals and gems needs a Fossicking Licence. These can be purchased from Miners Den (© 07 4051 4413) at 65 Anderson St, Cairns, which sells topographical maps, geological maps of gold-mining areas and other information. Licences are also available from businesses in Mount Surprise and Innot Hot Springs.

The Department of Natural Resources & Mines website, www.nrm.qld.gov.au, has fact sheets on the fossicking areas. Otherwise call into their office (© 07 4039 8382) at 5B Sheridan St, Cairns.

Pan for gold at the Tyrconnell Mine near Mt Mulligan

DENIS O'BYRNE

Organised Tours & Gear Hire

Mt Surprise Gems (© 07 4062 3055, mtsurprisegems@bigpond.com) in Mount Surprise sells permits and hires fossicking equipment. It also runs guided tours to O'Briens Creek including a tag-along option, and offers appraisal and faceting services.

The Tyrconnell Mine (© 07 4093 5177, www.tyrconnell.com.au) near Mt Mulligan lists panning for gold among its offerings.

Driving

Scenic Drives

Far North Queensland has plenty of breathtaking scenery but the roads aren't designed for enjoying it while you're driving along. In the predominantly hilly or mountainous terrain, where blind corners are all too common, it's best to concentrate on the way ahead, not gaze around at the countryside. Having said that, there are many drives that passengers will enjoy – provided motion sickness hasn't got the poor things heaving into a bag! The following is a small, hopefully representative selection.

- **Blencoe Falls Adventure.** The 71km bush road from Kennedy (near Cardwell) to Blencoe Falls is unsealed, steep, often rough, narrow, winding, little used and remote – all the ingredients necessary for a soft-core motoring adventure. En route you pass through cane fields and banana plantations, climb precipitous terrain clothed in wet tropical rainforest, and cross undulating hills covered in open eucalypt forest. Lookouts and a short rainforest walk add further interest. When dry, the road is passable with care to conventional vehicles with good ground clearance, but after rain only a 4WD will do. See the boxed text on p60.

- **Palmerston Hwy.** Leaving the Bruce Hwy just west of Innisfail, the sealed Palmerston Hwy provides a direct route from the coastal lowlands to Millaa Millaa, on the Atherton Tableland. For the first 28km this excellent road climbs through agricultural land and steep cow paddocks before entering the World Heritage rainforest of **Wooroonooran National Park**. In the next 5km or so the road passes walking tracks and picnic/camping areas, all of which are worth investigating (see the boxed text on p66).

What to Do

The forest ends just before the outskirts of Millaa Millaa, where you can take Tourist Route 9 on a circuit of three attractive waterfalls (see Millaa Millaa on ppp85-86).

- **Captain Cook Hwy.** Heading north from Cairns, the 37km section of highway between the turn-offs to Palm Cove and Port Douglas mainly winds through open eucalypt forest on the steep-sided **MacAlister Range**. Inspiring coastal views are a major feature of this drive, which takes you through part of the Wet Tropics WHA. En route are **Ellis** and **Wangetti beaches**, both of which are pretty much deserted during the week. Just before the turn-off to Wangetti Beach is **Hartley Crocodile Adventures**, where you can watch daily wildlife shows. **Rex Lookout**, a little further north, is a popular launching point for hang-gliders.

- **Palmer River Track.** The usual route to the historic **Palmer River Goldfield** is a 4WD track that leaves the Peninsula Developmental Rd 200m south of the Whites Creek crossing (17km south of the Palmer River Roadhouse). It's 79km from this unmarked turn-off to historic **Maytown** (see the boxed text on p96), and for much of the journey you follow the tops of narrow, forested ridgelines. The drive can get tedious, but the views as well as the destination make it worthwhile. Hazards include numerous blind crests and corners, bulldust holes, and steep ascents and descents. Allow three hours for the one-way trip, but don't consider it if rain is imminent anywhere in a wide radius because you can get cut off by rapidly rising rivers.

Other good scenic routes include the Cardwell Forest Drive near Cardwell; the Millaa Millaa Waterfall Circuit; the Old Palmerston Hwy between Millaa Millaa and Ravenshoe; the Old Bruce Hwy between El Arish and Innisfail; the Rex Hwy between Mossman and Mount Molloy; and the Peninsula Developmental Rd between Mount Molloy and Lakeland.

Four-Wheel Driving

Escapists who enjoy 4WD touring will find quite a bit to interest them in FNQ. Worthwhile routes where you're most unlikely to run into (or over) a Commodore include the Bloomfield Track, the road to Blencoe Falls, the Palmer River Track, the Black Mountain Rd, and the CREB Track between Daintree Village and the Bloomfield Rd near Wujal Wujal.

Apart from the CREB Track, which is recommended only for experts, experienced four-wheel drivers shouldn't find any of these routes particularly difficult once the country has dried out after the Wet. During the Dry you can expect a suite of hazards such as fallen trees (carry a small chainsaw), washouts and bulldust holes. Add significant rain and you'll also have flooded crossings, bog holes and steep slippery slopes to contend with. Even more heavy rain means that you probably won't be going anywhere for a while.

The Captain Cook Hwy north of Cairns

TOURISM QUEENSLAND

The CREB Track (p113, B6-A6)

Originally constructed as the service road for one of the Cairns Regional Electricity Board's power lines, the CREB Track provides a challenging 4WD route over the McDowall Range between Daintree Village and Ayton. It passes through World Heritage rainforest and eucalypt woodland, with some great views and the atmosphere of a remote forest environment. Just off the track is the impressive **Roaring Meg Falls**, where there is a QPWS campground by a magnificent swimming hole – the falls are along the road/walking track off to the left as you arrive at the campground, the swimming hole down the closed-off road to the right.

The ultra-steep clay slopes of the CREB Track render it unsuitable for novice four-wheel drivers. When dry, the track offers experts an enjoyable drive, but after a shower of rain – and it often rains in these parts – it becomes extremely difficult if not dangerous, and can be impassable. Many vehicles have had to be recovered at significant cost to the owners.

Even in dry conditions the track is unsuitable for vehicles lacking low-range gearing, good ground clearance and/or appropriate tyres. Heavily laden vehicles and trailers are not recommended. Parts of the track cross private land and travellers are requested to stay on the main track and leave gates as they find them.

The total distance from Daintree Village to the Bloomfield Rd between Wujal Wujal and Ayton is about 71km, of which 61km is 4WD only. Starting at the southern end, you head north on Upper Daintree Rd to the start of the track proper, which is just past the Daintree River Crossing, 10km from town. Be wary of the depth and flow of the river and be mindful of the likely presence of saltwater crocodiles.

Beyond here the track is almost unrelentingly steep, with many ascents, descents and creek crossings. The slopes in the northern section aren't as extreme as those in the south, but even so are no less treacherous when wet.

The track's northern end is 2.3km from the Bloomfield Crossing towards Ayton – it's the first major dirt road on your left, where the bitumen turns to gravel, and should have a stop sign.

Not surprisingly, the CREB track is closed during the wet season and at other times if the situation warrants it – check with the Wet Tropics Management Authority's Cairns office (☎ 07 4052 0555) for the latest. Visits to Roaring Meg Falls require a QPWS "permit to traverse" as well as a camping permit if you're staying overnight. The turn-off to the falls is about 49km from Daintree Village and 22km from the Bloomfield Rd, at the gate marking the northern boundary of the CREB Track proper.

Roaring Meg Falls is a major cultural site for the Kuku Yalanji people and their permission is also required to visit it – contact the Burungu Aboriginal Corporation on ☎ 07 4060 3106. This is a women's place and menfolk are requested to stay away from the immediate vicinity of the falls. The traditional owners are also concerned about safety issues (the crumbly granite around the falls is very slippery), and ask that all visitors stand well back from the edge.

What to Do

Roaring Meg Falls, an impressive sight just off the CREB Track

The secluded swimming hole at Roaring Meg Falls, an attractive place to cool down

DENIS O'BYRNE

Fallen trees are a common hazard on rainforest roads.

TOURISM QUEENSLAND

Far North Queensland offers good horse riding.

Motorcycling

The region's steep, curvy roads are seriously good fun for skilled bikers. On the outskirts of Cairns is a good appetiser in the form of the Lake Morris Rd with its long series of bends around the steep flanks of Mt Sheridan. The Kennedy Hwy between Cairns and Kuranda, and the Captain Cook Hwy between Palm Cove and Port Douglas are tightly sinuous routes. So too is the Rex Hwy where it winds upwards for 10km from sea level to the top of the Atherton Tableland. The broad, sweeping curves of the Palmerston Hwy between Innisfail and Millaa Millaa are also enjoyable.

Each of these roads offers a memorable experience, but they pale before the region's *pièce de résistance* – the scenic Gillies Hwy between Gordonvale and the Atherton Tableland. This corkscrew affair climbs 600m in 19km, with 236 tight, beautifully flowing bends. Great in a car, even better on a bike. The Mountain View Hotel at the bottom is a popular meeting point for bikers, some of whom turn up on "Gillies specials" modified with all the trick gear.

Rentals

The following places in Cairns rent bikes:
- **All Day Car Rental** (☎ 07 4031 3348)
- **Cairns Auz Motorbikes** (☎ 07 4052 1344)
- **Cairns Bike & Scooter Hire** (☎ 07 4031 4311)
- **Yahoo Bike Rentals** (☎ 07 4031 2379)

Organised Tours

There aren't many options but try the following:
- **Fair Dinkum Bike Tours** – trail-bike day tours and longer tours in forested country around Cairns, Daintree and beyond (☎ 07 4031 0540, www.FairDinkumBikeTours.com).
- **Stay Upright Adventure Tours** – one and two-day trail-bike tours around Cairns as well as eight-day trips from Cairns to Cape York (☎ 07 4032 1022, www.stayupright.com.au).

Horse Riding

Visitors who've brought their horses with them can ride the Bicentennial National Trail between Cooktown and Healesville, in Victoria (see boxed text). Otherwise there are a number of trail-ride operators who cater for expert and novice riders and, between them, offer a range of experiences on horseback.

Atherton Tableland
- **Springmount Station Horse Riding** – overnight rides as well as half-day and day trips on a cattle station on the western side of the Atherton Tableland (☎ 07 4093 4493, 1800 333 004, www.springmountstation.com)

Cairns Area
- **Blazing Saddles** – morning rides through forested country above Palm Cove (☎ 07 4059 0955, www.blazingsaddles.com.au)
- **Mount-N-Ride Adventures** – half-day, day and (for experts) private rides along rainforest trails through the Little Mulgrave Valley, near Gordonvale (☎ 07 4056 5406, mountnride@mountnride.com.au)

Cooktown

- **Hidden Valley Trail Rides** –
  morning, afternoon and evening rides
  on a variety of trails at Keatings Lagoon
  (✆ 07 4069 6073)

Mission Beach

- **Bush 'n' Beach** (✆ 07 4068 7893)

Port Douglas Area

- **Black Mountain Hideaway** –
  do the historic Bump Track and
  visit Big Mowbray Falls (✆ 07 4094 1101,
  www.blackmountainhideaway.com.au)

- **Mitchell River Trail Rides** –
  day and extended rides in a variety
  of environments west of Port Douglas
  (✆ 07 4094 3152,
  www.mitchellrivertrailrides.com.au)

- **Mowbray Valley Trails** –
  half-day and day rides including the
  Bump Track (✆ 07 4099 3268,
  www.mowbrayvalleytrailrides.com)

- **Wonga Beach Equestrian Centre** –
  morning and afternoon rides featuring
  beaches and rainforest near Daintree
  Village (✆ 07 4098 7583)

The Daintree

- **Cape Trib Horse Rides** – half-day
  rides incorporating beach, farming and
  rainforest environments (✆ 07 4098 0030,
  1800 111 124)

Caving

Caving opportunities are limited to the Chillagoe area, in the region's far west, where over 600 caves have been discovered in a belt of ancient coral reefs. A significant number of these are located within the Chillagoe-Mungana National Park, including the Queenslander Cave with its 10km of passageways – this is the state's largest cave system. Daily ranger-guided tours visit three show caves, and you can explore three others by yourself (see the Chillagoe section p101-102).

Other caves within the park may be visited by arrangement with the Chillagoe Caving Club, PO Box 92, Cairns 4870, www.chillagoe cavingclub.org.au, which has the required QPWS permit. Novices – or cavers who are not members of a recognised speleological association – must be accompanied by a member of the Chillagoe Caving Club.

The Bicentennial National Trail

Linking Cooktown with Healesville, near Melbourne, the 5330km Bicentennial National Trail is designed as a long-distance route for non-motorised trekkers on horseback, mountain bike and on foot. The trail is divided into 12 sections, with Section One (470km) taking you from Cooktown to Gunnawarra, a cattle-grazing property about 30km south of the little township of Mount Garnet. Mount Garnet is 44km west of Ravenshoe on the Kennedy Hwy (National Route 1).

Starting at Cooktown, the BNT heads south through World Heritage rainforest to Ayton, then crosses the range via the 4WD CREB Track (see p37). Some cyclists prefer to bypass the CREB Track by taking the main road via Cape Tribulation instead. This way is a lot easier apart from the road traffic, but it means missing out on Roaring Meg Falls and some terrific views.

At Mount Molloy you leave the mountains and rainforest and enter the western foothills with their cover of dry eucalypt forests. The section between Mount Molloy and Mutchilba is also difficult for cyclists, but once again there's an easier road option. Mutchilba is 10km east of Dimbulah on the Burke Developmental Rd.

It's recommended that horseback trekkers depart Cooktown in April/May so as to take advantage of the ready availability of surface water and grass. Horses brought up from the south should be given a fortnight to acclimatise.

For more information visit the BNT website, www.vicnet.net.au/~bnt/, or ring ✆ 1300 138 724. Each of the trail's 12 sections has its own guidebook, complete with maps.

Water-Based Activities

Great Barrier Reef Marine Park Authority zoning regulations restrict or ban certain activities such as shell collecting, boating and fishing in large areas of the marine park. Contact the GBRMPA in Townsville (℡ 1800 990 177) – or if in Cairns call in to the QPWS office – and ask them to send the fee zone map for your area of interest.

Complete coverage of the Reef between Cardwell and Cooktown is provided by three detailed 1:250,000 maps – *Innisfail MPZ27* (Cardwell to Gordonvale), *Cairns MPZ26* (Gordonvale to the Bloomfield River), and *Cooktown MPZ25* (Bloomfield River to Cape Melville). Also get hold of the GBRMPA's booklet *An Introduction to Using Our Great Barrier Reef.*

Visiting Small Islands

There's nothing quite like the unique atmosphere of a small island to recharge depleted mental batteries. Far North Queensland is blessed with a number of beautiful tropical islands where you can wander along deserted beaches pretending to be shipwrecked. Almost all are national parks and it's recommended that you contact the QPWS for advice before making independent visits to any 'off-the-beaten-track' island. Some are major bird-nesting sites where human activity is restricted during the breeding seasons.

A handful of islands boast comfortable resorts, while others have basic camping areas more suited to a Robinson Crusoe-like experience. Most resorts welcome day visitors, who may use their facilities – you can normally hire snorkelling gear, kayaks, catamarans and the like. Some have daily ferry services, while others are accessible by air and/or motor launch. In the case of uninhabited islands, you'll generally have to hire a water taxi (where available) or seaplane, or paddle out to them in a kayak.

Walking along Cardwell's main street you can see the rugged outline of Hinchinbrook Island beckoning from just 5km offshore. The island is a national park and is uninhabited apart from a small resort at the northern end. Accessible by ferry from Cardwell, Hinchinbrook has one of Queensland's best wilderness walks – the 32km Thorsborne Trail.

Look north from Cardwell's jetty and you'll see a number of mostly distant islands rising enticingly from the sea. Camping is permitted on Goold Island, which is off the northern end of Hinchinbrook Island, and in the Family Islands off Mission Beach. The latter group includes Dunk and Bedarra islands, both with resorts. Day-trippers can visit Dunk Island but not Bedarra.

There are more small islands up towards Innisfail, where several members of the Barnard Group have camping sites. Continuing north you come to the Frankland Group off the

TOURISM QUEENSLAND

Fitzroy Island, a popular excursion from Cairns

What to Do

mouth of the Russell River. This stunning area is visited daily by boat cruises operating from Cairns. They'll drop you off on Russell Island, where camping is permitted.

Ferry services link Cairns with the resorts on Fitzroy and Green islands, both of which are about 50 minutes from town. Green Island is a postcard-perfect coral cay, which is probably why it attracts two million visitors annually. The much larger Fitzroy Island will appeal to those who'd prefer to avoid crowds.

North of Cairns you can visit Michaelmas Cay (famous for its bird life) from Palm Cove, and the Low Isles from Port Douglas; there's an exclusive resort on Double Island, near Palm Cove. Snapper Island, off the mouth of the Daintree River, can be reached by kayak and has camping facilities. Further north, near Cedar Bay, the Hope Islands are accessible by water taxi from Ayton, and camping is permitted here as well.

Although out of date, Lonely Planet's *Islands of Australia's Great Barrier Reef* (1998) contains plenty of useful information for visits to the islands. See also Books & Magazines p24.

Fishing

It's probably fair to say that most anglers visiting FNQ want to catch a large barramundi. These magnificent sport fish are noted for their explosive leaps as they try to throw the hook. They can be caught off rocky headlands such as Buchan Point (near Cairns), and in lagoons, freshwater streams and estuaries. Lake Tinaroo, a large irrigation dam on the Atherton Tableland, is famous for its barra fishing. Generally the best months are September to May inclusive, although a three-month closed season applies from October to February to all habitats except Lake Tinaroo.

Another popular target is the Spanish mackerel, a large game species that hunts these waters in voracious packs between April and October. Mackerel can be caught around inshore islands, rocky headlands and jetties wherever there's a current. Hot spots include the Palm Cove jetty, the Cooktown wharf, and the rocky shoreline below Rex Lookout on the Captain Cook Hwy between Cairns and Port Douglas. If the Spaniards aren't cooperating you might have more luck with one of their smaller relatives – the grey, school, shark and spotted mackerel.

The region has numerous estuaries and these offer plenty of fishing potential – just about all FNQ's coastal towns have estuaries (Cairns has two). However, dense mangrove forests restrict access to the water's edge, and of course there are crocodiles to think about. Barracuda, bream, flathead, grunter, queenfish, salmon and whiting are common catches at river mouths, while barramundi, fingermark, mangrove jack, salmon and trevally are found further up. Live bait, particularly prawns and yabbies, gives the best results.

Estuaries are also home to the prized mud crab (commonly referred to as "muddies") and these can be caught in enclosed traps baited with 'off' lamb chops, fish frames and the like. Pots should be set on a muddy bottom on the edge of the mangroves as the tide is rising, and checked when it's falling.

Freshwater habitats upstream from the estuaries are home to yet another suite of species including barramundi, jungle perch, mangrove jack, sooty grunter and tarpon. These fish are most active during the wet season, and the best places to try are where feeder creeks enter the main stream after a good rain – all that tucker in the water is a powerful attraction for predatory fish. Shallow or surface lures, flies and poppers are used here.

Still in freshwater habitats, redclaw crayfish grow to 300g and can be caught in pots baited with rotting meat, old potatoes and so on – it appears that they'll eat almost anything as long as it's decaying! Try where there are submerged logs and other places for the redclaws to hide in, as they don't dig burrows like other yabbies.

While river and estuary fishing can be very productive and great fun, the reef is where it all happens if the number of charter boats is anything to go by. Reef fishing yields a host of species including cod, coral trout, small and large-mouthed nannygai, red bass, red emperor, reef mangrove jack, snapper, spangled emperor and turrum.

There's no shortage of boat hire places – see Yachting & Boating later in this chapter. Being sensible folk, boat hirers won't let customers take their tinnies out to the reef. This means that if you want to get among the action you'll probably have to join a fishing charter. This won't necessarily blow your budget as business is competitive and prices are generally very reasonable.

Crocodile Safety

ROB VAN DRIESUM

Estuarine or saltwater crocodiles (*Crocodylus porosus*) are common residents of the wetlands of coastal FNQ. They live mainly in the tidal reaches of rivers, but also occur in freshwater habitats considerable distances inland and around offshore islands. Saltwater crocodiles (or "salties") are most active at night, particularly during their breeding season from September to April.

In the eyes of a large saltie a human is prey and there have been a number of attacks across northern Australia in recent years, several of them fatal. Visitors are urged to observe the following common-sense guidelines where crocodiles are present:

- Observe warning signs – do not swim in crocodile habitat.
- Stay well back from the water's edge when fishing or carrying out any other activity – don't stand on overhanging branches.
- Do not clean fish at boat ramps or other places where people gather.
- Keep arms and legs inside the boat.
- Camp at least 50m back from the water's edge and, if possible, 5m above the water.
- Do not leave food scraps around your camp.
- Do not feed crocodiles or interfere with them in any way.

Last but by no means least is Cairns's reputation as an international game-fishing centre. May to September is the season for small black marlin and sailfish – exciting stuff on light tackle – while September to December is the giant black marlin season. It might take a while to save the price of a charter trip in pursuit of giant blacks, but the experience will almost certainly be worth it. An enthusiastic big-game fisherman, the late movie star Lee Marvin was hooked on black marlin. He visited Cairns annually from 1973 to his death in 1987 for this sole purpose.

Information

No licence is required for recreational fishing in FNQ's freshwater and tidal waters (with the exception of Lake Tinaroo, see pp80-82) but there are a number of rules and regulations. The *Guide to Recreational Boating & Fishing in Queensland* – a joint effort by Maritime Safety Queensland (℡ 07 3860 3500, www.msq.qld.gov.au) and the Department of Primary Industries & Fisheries (℡ 07 3404 6999, www.dpi.qld.gov.au/fishweb) – gives a wealth of information on a range of topics such as bag and size limits, closed seasons, closed waters and 'no take' species. It's widely available from visitor information centres, QPWS offices and tackle and boat shops.

There aren't any fishing guidebooks specific to the coast and waterways between Cardwell and Cooktown. However, if you peruse *Bransford's Guide to Fishing – Cairns to Cape York*, the annual *North Australian Fish Finder* and Explore Australia's *The Queensland Fishing Atlas*, you'll find plenty of useful information on the area in question.

VIEWFINDER

Fishing Charters

The choice of operators is overwhelming, particularly in Cairns. Between them they offer all manner of experiences, from half-day crabbing trips to extended trips in search of big game species:

Cairns – River & Estuary Fishing

- **All Tackle Sportfishing** – rivers and inlets near Cairns and Daintree (℡ 07 4034 2550, www.alltacklesportsfishing.com.au)
- **Billfish Sports Fishing** – various forms of deep sea and estuary fishing (℡ 07 4031 4444)
- **Cairns Calm Water Fishing Charters** – half-day trips on Trinity Inlet (℡ 0417 441 239)
- **Cairns Fishing Charters** – estuary trips (℡ 07 4035 1179)
- **Cairns Reel Sport Fishing Charters** (℡ 07 4045 1692)
- **Catcha Crab** – crabbing trips on Trinity Inlet (℡ 07 4051 7992, www.catcha-crab.com.au)
- **Eco Sportsfisher** – river, estuarine and coastal locations (℡ 07 4057 6665)
- **Fish Hunter Sportfishing Charters** (℡ 0417 707 787)
- **Fish Tales Charters** – sports fishing trips on rivers and inlets near Cairns and Daintree (℡ 07 4045 0234, www.fishtales.com.au)
- **Fishing the North** – half and full-day trips on rivers and estuaries (℡ 07 4045 2987)
- **Fishing the Tropics** – reef, estuary and river trips in the Cairns and Daintree areas (℡ 07 4058 1820, www.fishingthetropics.com.au)
- **Great Day Fishing & Crabbing Tours** (℡ 0412 967 172)
- **Paradise Sportfishing Adventures** – estuary and river fishing (℡ 07 4055 6088, 0408 774 088)
- **Tropical Boat Charters** – estuary and river fishing (℡ 07 4036 2009, tropicalure@picknowl.com.au)

Cairns – Reef & Game Fishing

- **Aqua-Cat Charters** – based at Clifton Beach (℡ 07 4059 1500)
- **Barrier Reef Billfish & Dive** – based at Yorkeys Knob (℡ 07 4055 8833, www.gamefish.com.au)
- **Billfish Sports Fishing** – various forms of deep sea and estuary fishing (℡ 07 4031 4444)
- **Blue Whaler Reef Fishing Charters** (℡ 07 4033 7140)
- **Cairns Reef Charter Services** – various forms of fishing between Cardwell and Cooktown, and beyond (℡ 07 4031 4742, www.luxuryboatcharters.com.au)
- **Cairns Sport Fishing** – heavy and light tackle and fly fishing on day and extended charters (℡ 07 4031 6516, www.cairnssportfishing.com.au)
- **Fishing Cairns** – everything from fly to heavy tackle fishing, as well as extended charters (℡ 07 4038 1144, www.fishingcairns.com.au)
- **Fishing the Tropics** – reef, estuary and river trips in the Cairns and Daintree areas (℡ 07 4058 1820, www.fishingthetropics.com.au)
- **Floreat Reef Charter** (℡ 07 4095 3641, floreatreefcharters@bigpond.com)
- **Moana Charters** – variety of fishing experiences from Cairns and Cooktown, as well as sole charters up to 14 days (℡ 07 4045 2813, 0413 054 031, www.moanacharters.com)
- **Powerplay Charters** – reef and game fishing (both light and heavy tackle) from Yorkeys Knob (℡ 07 4053 7015, 1800 002 322 mvpowerplay@austarnet.com.au)
- **Sea Venture Charters** – light and heavy tackle (℡ 07 4035 2352, www.seaventurecharters.com.au)
- **Serious Adventures** – self-drive or guided island, reef and headland trips (℡ 0418 772 751)

continued next page

What to Do

Fishing Charters *continued from previous page*

- **Trinity Sport Fishing Charter** – based at Trinity Beach (☏ 07 4055 6688)
- **Viking II** – light and heavy tackle (☏ 07 4032 5444, www.australianmarlin.com)
- **VIP Fishing & Game Boat Services** – various forms of fishing from fly to heavy tackle (☏ 07 4031 4355, www.cairnsvisitorcentre.com)
- **Wild Turkey** – light and heavy tackle (☏ 0400 015 902)

Cape Tribulation
- **Cape Tribulation Fishing Charters** (☏ 07 4098 9237)
- **Cape Tribulation Wilderness Cruises & Reef Fishing** (☏ 07 4098 9052, www.capetribcruises.com)
- **Daintree Coast Reef Fishing** (☏ 07 4090 7201)
- **Daintree River Fishing & Photography** (☏ 07 4090 7776, daveandsandra@ledanet.com.au)

Cardwell
- **Aquarius Charters** – reef and light game fishing trips in the Hinchinbrook area (☏ 07 4066 2227)
- **Hinchinbrook Explorer Fishing & Eco Tours** – reef, river and estuary trips including Mission Beach (☏ 07 4088 6154, www.hexplorer.com.au)
- **Reel to Reel Sportfishing Charters** (☏ 0417 717 722)

- **Un-Reel Sports Fishing Adventures** – based at Kennedy, with lure and fly fishing (☏ 07 4066 0032, www.un-reel-sports-fishing-adventures.com.au)

Cooktown
- **Cooktown Catch-a-Crab** – half-day crabbing trips (☏ 07 4069 6289, cathyadams@fni.aunz.com)
- **Cooktown Reef Charters** – full-day and extended charters for bottom and sports fishing (☏ 07 4069 5519, slippery@tpg.com.au)
- **Gone Fishing** – half and full-day trips on the Annan, Endeavour and McIvor rivers (☏ 07 4069 5980, www.fishingcooktown.com)
- **Reel River Sport Fishing** – all forms of estuary fishing on half and full-day tours (☏ 07 4069 5346)

Innisfail
- **Barrajack Encounters** – river and estuary trips (☏ 07 4061 3790)
- **Bramston Beach Fishing Charters** (☏ 07 4067 4186)

Mission Beach
- **Fishin' Mission** – reef and island trips (☏ 07 4088 6121)

Port Douglas
- **Coral Sea Adventures** (☏ 07 4099 3391)
- **Doreen Too** (☏ 07 4099 3391)

No shortage of recreational fishing charters, in this case in Cairns

DENIS O'BYRNE

- **Dragon Lady** – game fishing
  (☎ 07 4099 4281,
  www.gamefishingportdouglas.com)
- **Fish 1 Sportfishing** – half and full-day
  estuary and reef trips (07 4094 1671)
- **Joe Joe Charters** – various styles of
  fishing around Port Douglas and
  further afield (☎ 0418 772 459,
  www.mvjoejoe.com)
- **MV Norseman** – day trips
  (☎ 07 4099 5031)
- **Out 'n' About** – half and full-day estuary and reef trips (☎ 07 4098 5204)
- **Phantom Charters** – light-tackle
  game fishing (☎ 07 4094 1220,
  www.phantomcharters.com)
- **Restless Fishing Charters**
  (☎ 0427 212 444)
- **Trinity Sportfishing** – half-day estuary
  trips (☎ 07 4099 5031)
- **Tropical Fishing & Eco Tours** –
  reef and estuary (☎ 07 4099 4272,
  outerreef@bigpond.com)
- **True Blue Fishing Charters** – mud
  crabbing and estuary fishing
  (☎ 07 4099 4966,
  trueblue@austarnet.com.net)
- **Weejock Charters** – game fishing
  (☎ 0419 942 004, www.weejock.com.au)

The Daintree
- **Fishing on the Daintree** – half and full-
  day sports fishing trips (☎ 07 4090 7638)
- **Fafun** – estuaries, rivers and inshore
  reefs, as well as freshwater streams
  (☎ 0427 776 787,
  fafun@ledanet.com.au)
- **Still Cruizin** (☎ 07 4061 4334)

Lake Tinaroo
- **Tinaroo Waters Birds & Barra**
  (☎ 07 4095 8425,
  www.tinaroowaters.com.au)
- **Gerry's Wildlife Cruise & Fishing**
  (☎ 07 4095 3658)

National fishing magazines such as *Modern Fishing* regularly have features on FNQ. Also check *The Cairns Post's* Friday edition, which includes two or three pages of regional fishing news. *Fish & Boat* is a monthly newspaper devoted to FNQ's fishing and boating scene.

Last but no means least, Les Marsh's *Fishing Cairns* website (www.fishingcairns.com.au) is an absolute mine of information.

Fish Farms
Serious anglers may scoff and turn their noses up, but if all else fails you should be able to catch a feed at one of FNQ's fish farms. Fishing tackle and bait are normally available:

- **Barramundi Gardens** – on the Rex Hwy near Mossman (☎ 07 4094 1293)
- **Fish-O-Rama** – between El Arish and Mission Beach (☎ 07 4068 5350, www.fish-o-rama.com.au)
- **Tarzali Lakes Fishing Park** – between Malanda and Millaa Millaa on the Atherton Tableland (☎ 07 4097 2713)

Diving & Snorkelling
The Great Barrier Reef is a huge attraction for divers and snorkellers, with comfortable water temperatures and good visibility year round. There are numerous commercial operators waiting to take you out to where the action is. See the Reef Trips boxed text on pp48-49 for contact details, as well as the list of dedicated scuba diving schools on pp46-47, though these lists are by no means exhaustive.

Costs vary enormously. To give a rough idea, in 2004 Cairns Dive Centre (CDC) was charging $75/120 for a basic day's snorkelling/diving trip (two dives by certified divers) in a maximum group of 25 passengers. It also had a live-aboard dive option costing $341/451 for two/three days.

Most day trips departing from Cairns concentrate on the so-called Inter-Reef Gardens with their shallow coral growths that resemble exotic gardens of infinite variety. Further out is the Outer Reef with its exciting mix of dramatic underwater topography, coral gardens and huge schools of pelagic fishes. On a three-day trip you should be able to log a total of at least 10 day and night dives, each of which will have something different to offer.

North of Mossman are the aptly named Ribbon Reefs, which can be explored on extended

Diver peering through a school of bait fish

Scuba training

trips from Cairns and Port Douglas. This area, known for its wall dives and diversity of marine life, is on the edge of the continental shelf. It includes the famous Cod Hole up near Lizard Island, where you can dive with massive but fortunately placid potato cod. Beyond the continental shelf, the scattered reefs of the Coral Sea feature huge drop-offs, usually excellent visibility (up to 40m) and numerous sharks. These reefs can also be visited on extended trips.

Information

The Diving Cairns website, www.divingcairns.com, has a wealth of useful information.

Reef Teach (© 07 4031 7794) at 14 Spence St in Cairns conducts entertaining lectures nightly except Sunday on the dynamics of the Great Barrier Reef. If you want to understand more about this fascinating ecosystem then this is for you – not only will you learn something but you'll have a good time doing it. Lectures start at 6.15pm and cost $13.

Scuba Diving Schools

It's not necessary to be a scuba diver to enjoy the Great Barrier Reef, as there is more than enough marine life between the surface and a depth of 4m to keep you enthralled for hours just snorkelling. Having said that, scuba diving opens up a whole new world, and the quickest way through the door is to take an introductory or resort dive.

You may enjoy your introductory dive so much that you decide to enrol in a course and earn an approved diving certificate. This is subject to a medical examination as some conditions (e.g. asthma, epilepsy) do not lend themselves to safe diving.

Full-time diving courses take up to six days and consist of instruction in the classroom and swimming pool followed by dives on the Reef. Many operators have live-aboard vessels, which is the way to go if you can afford it.

Once you have your certificate, dive operators all over the world will be happy to do business with you. The best known international certificates are issued by PADI (Professional Association of Diving Instructors). FAUI (Federation of Australian Underwater Instructors) is also recognised overseas.

The following dive schools offer courses leading to open-water certification. Most of the island resorts offer diver training as an activity for their guests:

Cairns

- **Aquapro Diving Services** (© 07 4032 3019, www.aquaprodive.com)
- **Cairns Dive Centre** (© 07 4051 0294, www.cairnsdive.com.au)
- **Cairns Reef** Dive (© 07 4051 0294, www.cairnsreefdive.com.au)
- **Deep Sea Divers Den** (© 07 4046 7333, www.divers-den.com)
- **Dive 7 Seas** (© 07 4041 2700)
- **Divers Net** (© 07 4041 5977)
- **Mike Ball Dive Expeditions** (© 07 4031 5484, www.mikeball.com)
- **Pro-Dive Cairns** (© 07 4031 5255, www.prodive-cairns.com.au)
- **Reef Magic Cruises** (© 07 4031 1588, www.reefmagiccruises.com)
- **Reef Encounters & Compass Cruises** (© 07 4051 5777, 1800 GO REEF, www.reeftrip.com)

- **Seahorse Sail & Dive** (✆ 07 4041 1919, www.seahorsedive.com.au)
- **Spirit of Freedom** (✆ 07 4040 6450, www.spiritoffreedom.com.au)
- **Scuba Schools International** (✆ 07 4044 4999)
- **Seaquest ADV** (✆ 07 4046 7333)
- **Taka Dive** (✆ 07 4051 8722, www.takadive.com.au)

Mission Beach

- **Calypso Dive** (✆ 07 4068 8432, www.calypsodive.com)

Port Douglas

- **Haba Dive & Snorkel** (✆ 07 4099 5254, www.habadive.com.au)
- **Quicksilver Dive** (✆ 07 4099 5050, www.quicksilverdive.com.au)
- **Sheridans** (✆ 07 4099 5770, sheridandive@austarnet.com.au)
- **Tech Dive Academy** (✆ 07 4099 6880, www.tech-dive-academy.com)
- **VIP Diving Services** (✆ 07 4099 4890, info@portdouglasdive.com.au)

Swimming

There are many excellent swimming beaches, some of which are easy to get to while others require a degree of determination. The more popular ones (e.g. Port Douglas and Cairns's northern beaches) are patrolled by life-savers daily either throughout the year or from September to May (the stinger season, see boxed text p50).

During this period you can either swim inside stinger-resistant enclosures, or head for the nearest crocodile-free water hole. Areas upstream of waterfalls or significant rapids are usually safe from crocodiles but there's no guarantee of this – always seek local advice before plunging into remote pools.

Beaches for Naturists

There are no authorised nudist beaches in FNQ. However, Cairns does have an *unofficial* nude beach at Buchan Point, between Palm Cove and Ellis Beach. The parking area is the first one on your right past Buchan Point heading north on the Captain Cook Hwy.

Water Holes

The crystal-clear freshwater streams that flow down the mountainsides create plunge pools that often make good swimming holes, and FNQ is blessed with many of them. While there are no stingers here, flash floods can result from heavy rain over the catchment. Get out fast if the water level starts to rise.

Also be aware that some river systems, such as the Mulgrave, are the home of bullrout (a freshwater stinging fish). Bullrout are camouflaged, bottom-dwelling fish and footwear with stout soles is recommended as protection from the poisonous spines on their fins. If stung, elevate the wounded area and seek medical assistance. As with saltwater crocodiles, seek local advice and observe warning signs before entering the water.

The following swimming holes are particularly popular and/or rewarding:

- Lake Placid (Cairns), p71
- Crystal Cascades (Cairns), p74
- Malanda Falls, p83
- Millaa Millaa Falls, p85
- Alligators Nest (near Tully), p61
- Lake Eacham (near Malanda), p80
- Babinda Boulders, p68
- Behana Gorge (near Gordonvale), p68
- Goldsborough Valley (near Gordonvale), p68
- Cardwell Forest Drive (several holes), p58
- Roaring Meg (CREB Track), p37

Whale-Watching

Humpback whales are often seen from tourist craft and islands off the FNQ coast on their annual winter breeding and calving migration from Antarctic waters. Sadly, however, the whales are too dispersed in this area to make specialised whale-watching tours viable.

Dwarf minke whales are frequent visitors to the reef between March and October, with June/July being the busiest period. These small (6-8m) baleen whales are most commonly sighted around the Ribbon Reefs, out from Port Douglas. Groups of five or six may be seen, but singles and pairs are more usual.

Port Douglas-based dive operators Poseidon Outer Reef Cruises (✆ 07 4099 4772) and Undersea Explorer (✆ 07 4099 5911) have permits to take people diving and snorkelling with dwarf minke whales. Check with the visitor information centre in Port Douglas for others, if any.

Reef Trips

There are many ways to explore the Great Barrier Reef and you don't always have to go diving or snorkelling to do so. There's something to suit everyone, particularly in Cairns where a veritable armada of craft of all shapes and sizes offers a variety of options. These include charters and scheduled day, overnight and extended trips by cruiser, wave-piercing catamaran or yacht.

Some operators cater for small groups (maximum 25) and have relatively high passenger/crew ratios. At the other end of the scale are the fast catamarans that carry upwards of 300 passengers. The latter, such as Cairns-based Sunlover, tie up to huge pontoons where underwater observatories, glass-bottom boats and/or semi-submersibles allow non-divers and snorkellers to view the marine world without getting their feet wet. Sunlover also has an option whereby you don a helmet connected to a surface air supply and go for a walk along a submerged platform. Scenic helicopter flights are available from some pontoons.

Costs vary depending on the service. To give an indication, in 2004 Sunlover was charging $179 per person including the glass-bottom boat/semi-submersible option. Extras were guided snorkelling tours ($20), the 'underwater walk' ($129) and an introductory or certified scuba dive (both $109).

See the main Diving & Snorkelling text for other options.

Cairns

Big Cat, Great Adventures, Quicksilver and Sunlover run high-speed catamarans with passenger capacities exceeding 300.

- **Barrier Reef Billfish & Dive**
  (✆ 07 4055 8833, www.gamefish.com.au)
- **Big Cat Green Island Reef Cruises**
  (✆ 07 4051 0444,
  www.bigcat-cruises.com.au)
- **Cairns Dive Centre** (✆ 07 4051 0294,
  www.cairnsdive.com.au)
- **Cairns Reef Charter Services**
  (✆ 07 4031 4742,
  www.luxuryboatcharters.com.au)
- **Cairns Reef Dive** (✆ 07 4051 0294,
  www.cairnsreefdive.com.au)
- **Coral Sea Diving Company**
  (✆ 07 4041 2024,
  www.coralseadiving.com.au)
- **Coral Princess Cruises** (✆ 07 4040 9999,
  www.coralprincess.com.au)
- **Deep Sea Divers Den** (✆ 07 4046 7333,
  www.divers-den.com)
- **Down Under Cruise & Dive**
  (✆ 07 4052 8300, 1800 079 099,
  www.downunderdive.com.au)
- **Floreat Reef Charter** (✆ 07 4095 3641,
  floreatreefcharters@bigpond.com)

Reef pontoon off Cairns

TOURISM QUEENSLAND

- **Frankland Islands Cruise & Dive** (✆ 07 4031 6300, www.franklandislands.com)
- **Great Adventures Reef & Island Cruises** (✆ 07 4044 9944, www.greatadventures.com.au)
- **Mike Ball Dive Expeditions** (✆ 07 4031 5484, www.mikeball.com)
- **Nimrod Explorer Ventures** (✆ 07 4031 5566, www.explorerventures.com)
- **Ocean Spirit Cruises** (✆ 07 4031 2920, www.oceanspirit.com.au)
- **Passions of Paradise** (✆ 07 4050 0676, www.passionsofparadise.com)
- **Phantom Charters** (✆ 07 4094 1220, www.phantomcharters.com)
- **Powerplay Charters** (✆ 07 4053 7015, 1800 002 322, mvpowerplay@austarnet.com.au)
- **Pro-Dive Cairns** (✆ 07 4031 5255, www.prodive-cairns.com.au)
- **Quicksilver** (✆ 07 4087 2100, www.quicksilver-cruises.com)
- **Reef Encounters & Compass Cruises** (✆ 07 4051 5777, www.reeftrip.com)
- **Reef Magic Cruises** (✆ 07 4031 1588, www.reefmagiccruises.com)
- **Ruben Jane Charters** (✆ 07 4036 0777, www.rubenjane.com)
- **Seahorse Sail & Dive** (✆ 07 4041 1919, www.seahorsedive.com.au)
- **Spirit of Freedom** (✆ 07 4040 6450, www.spiritoffreedom.com.au)
- **Sea Venture Charters** (✆ 07 4035 2352, www.seaventurecharters.com.au)
- **Sunlover Cruises** (✆ 07 4050 1333, www.sunlover.com.au)
- **Taka Dive** (✆ 07 4051 8722, www.takadive.com.au)
- **Tusa Dive** (✆ 07 4040 6464, www.tusadive.com)

- **Vagabond Dive 'N Sail** (✆ 07 4031 0784, www.vagabond-dive.com)
- **Wild Turkey Charters** (✆ 0400 015 902)

Cape Tribulation
- **Odyssey H2O** (Coconut Beach Rainforest Lodge ✆ 07 4098 0033, www.voyages.com.au)
- **Rum Runner Cape Tribulation** (✆ 07 4098 9249, www.rumrunner.com.au)

Mission Beach
- **Blue Thunder Cruises** (✆ 07 4068 7289)
- **Calypso Dive** (✆ 07 4068 7289, www.calypsodive.com)
- **Mission Beach Dive Charters** (✆ 07 4068 7277)
- **QuickCat Cruises** (✆ 07 4068 7289)

Port Douglas
- **Aristocat** (✆ 07 4099 4727, www.aristocat.com.au)
- **Calypso** (✆ 07 4099 3377, www.calypsocharters.com.au)
- **Haba Dive** (✆ 07 4099 5254, www.habadive.com.au)
- **Poseidon Outer Reef Cruises** (✆ 07 4099 4772, www.poseidon-cruises.com.au)
- **Quicksilver** (✆ 07 4087 2100, www.quicksilver-cruises.com.au)
- **Sailaway** (✆ 07 4099 4772, www.sailawayportdouglas.com)
- **Tech Dive Academy** (✆ 07 4099 6880, www.tech-dive-academy.com)
- **Undersea Explorer** (✆ 07 4099 5911, www.undersea.com.au)
- **Wavelength Reef Charters** (✆ 07 4099 5031) – specialises in snorkelling
- **Weejock Charters** (✆ 0419 942 004, www.weejock.com.au)

Killer Jellyfish

The coastal waters of FNQ are at their most inviting during the period from early October to late April, when the weather is hot and muggy. However, only fools and ignorant tourists enter the sea at this time of year without wearing full-body protection against potentially deadly jellyfish.

There are two dangerous species of box jellyfish, also called stingers, in these waters – **chironex box jellyfish** (*Chironex fleckeri*) and **irukandji** (*Carukia barnesi*). Both are transparent, thus virtually invisible. You won't know they're there until you feel the pain that indicates you've made contact with the stinging cells in their tentacles.

Chironex is by far the largest and most common of the two. It has a circular body up to 300mm across from which hang as many as 50 venom-charged tentacles up to 3m long. The pain of a severe sting is immediate and incapacitating, and attempting to wipe any tentacles remaining on the skin will only make matters worse. Severe stings may cause the victim's breathing to cease or their heart to stop.

The tiny (to 20mm across) irukandji is most common in the warmer months, but occurs year round on reefs, around islands and off mainland beaches. The pain of its sting is only minor at first, but after 20-40 minutes comes agonising muscular pain, headache, vomiting and sweating. The venom can cause the victim's blood pressure to rise to a potentially fatal level.

A lycra stinger suit is a good idea if you must swim in the sea during the stinger season

Swim Safely

Short of staying out of the water, the best way to avoid stingers is to do your cooling-off in a freshwater stream. Observe the following simple precautions if you intend to swim in the sea during the stinger season:

- Observe warning signs – don't enter the water when the beach is closed.
- Swim only at patrolled beaches, and stay between the red and yellow flags.
- Swim in stinger-resistant enclosures where these are provided – note that stinger-resistant doesn't mean stinger-proof.
- Wear full protective clothing such as a wetsuit or lycra stinger suit.

First Aid

The following are the first aid priorities for a severe sting. Note that vinegar (any kind will do) should always be carried as a first-aid treatment for chironex and irukandji stings. Vinegar stops further discharge of venom from the stinging cells, thus preventing the pain from getting worse. First-aid vinegar containers are installed on some of the more popular beaches.

Stinger first aid consists of vinegar, which is provided at some beaches (here at Noah Beach)

- Remove the victim from the water – do not attempt to remove any tentacles that may be stuck to the skin, as this will only cause more venom to be injected.
- Call for medical assistance – dial ☎ 000.
- Provide CPR if required.
- Pour vinegar onto the stung area for 30 seconds.
- Transport the victim to medical attention.

Seek medical advice immediately in the event of a suspected irukandji sting. Don't wait for the symptoms to manifest themselves.

For more on stingers, visit www.marinestingers.com.

Canoeing & White-Water Kayaking

During the dry season there are plenty of options for short flat-water paddles on the lower sections of rivers like the Mulgrave, Tully and Barron. The Atherton Tableland has lakes Barrine, Eacham, Koombooloomba and Tinaroo, all of which offer enjoyable canoeing. Barrine, Eacham and Koombooloomba feature rainforested shores where there's a good chance of seeing wildlife.

Thanks to the daily release of water for hydroelectric power generation, the Barron and Tully rivers are year-round white-water venues, with grade 5 rapids in flood conditions. During the Wet, experienced kayakers can choose from numerous rain-dependent rivers.

In March-April (provided there's enough water) you can paddle all the way down the Walsh from Dimbulah to Chillagoe. There's also the Mitchell with its long fishing holes near Mount Molloy and Mount Carbine. On the Atherton Tableland the Barron and North Johnstone rivers have potential – at moderate water levels, the Barron between Mareeba and Kuranda is suitable for skilled canoeists.

Far North Queensland's most popular canoeing and white-water kayaking venue is the Mulgrave River, near Gordonvale. Except during flood conditions, the section from the Ross & Locke recreation area on the Gillies Hwy to the Bruce Hwy Bridge is suitable for novices, and there are more challenging sections upstream. After about September portaging is

Crystal Cascades, a delightful swimming spot near Cairns

ROB VAN DRIESUM

required around shallow sections. Apart from the usual hazards, you need to be mindful of low bridges on this river.

Information & Canoe/Kayak Hire

The Tinaroo Canoe Club (www.tinaroo.canoe.org.au) is an excellent source of information on the rivers that rise on the Atherton Tableland. Contact office bearers Peter McAulay (℡ 07 4095 4514), Rachel Bernays (bernays@austarnet.com.au) or Terry McClelland (tkmccl@qld.chariot.net.au).

Experienced Cairns kayaker Struan Lamont (℡ 07 4034 2768) is also happy to provide advice to visitors.

Kayak, Canoe Hire & Sales (℡ 07 4045 2864) in Cairns rents kayaks and canoes.

Sea Kayaking

With its numerous small islands and varied coastline of rocky headlands, secluded coves and long, sweeping beaches, FNQ has much to offer the sea kayaker. Between Cardwell and Cairns is a plethora of islands that are ideal for kayaking around. There aren't so many north of Cairns, but as a consolation the coast beyond the Daintree River is much less populated.

The Daintree coast, Snapper Island (near the mouth of the Daintree River), the Port Douglas area, the beaches and islands around Mission Beach, and Hinchinbrook Island (a real kayaking gem) can all be explored on guided kayaking tours. Mission Beach is the place to go if you want to do a tour of three days or more, otherwise the options are mainly restricted to half-day and day paddles.

Alternatively, experienced kayakers can rent a craft and do their own thing. What better way to spend your annual leave than paddling along the coast from Cardwell to Cairns, or Cairns to Cooktown? Just beware of crocodiles in estuarine waters, particularly north of Port Douglas (see the boxed text on p42).

The best conditions for sea kayaking occur during the winter months, when daytime temperatures are at their most comfortable and there is still plenty of water in the creeks. The southeast trade winds can be a nuisance, but they're not so bad if you're heading north. Spring brings calmer conditions, but visitors from southern climes may find the weather in late-October/November a little too warm for comfort. Stingers are another turn-off late in the year!

Organised Tours & Kayak Hire

Cairns

- **Palm Cove Watersports** – sunrise and sunset paddles, and half-day sea-kayaking trips to Double Island from Palm Cove; kayak hire available (✆ 0402 861 011, www.palmcovewatersports.com)
- **Raging Thunder** – tours around Fitzroy Island (✆ 07 4030 7990, www.ragingthunder.com.au)

Cape Tribulation

- **Cape Tribulation Sea Kayaking** – half and full-day trips around the cape; kayak hire available (✆ 07 4098 0077, www.tropicalparadise.com.au)
- **Paddle Trek** – morning and afternoon trips around the Cape Tribulation coast (✆ 07 4098 0040, www.daintreecoast.com.au)
- **Tropical Sea Kayaks** – overnight trips down the coast from Cow Bay to beautiful Snapper Island, near the Daintree River Mouth (Crocodylus Village ✆ 07 4098 9166, crocodylus@austarnet.com.au)

Mission Beach

- **Coral Sea Kayaking** – half-day trips along the coast, full-day tours to Dunk Island, three-day trips around the Family Group and extended trips to Hinchinbrook Island; kayak hire available (✆ 07 4068 9154, 0419 782 453, www.coralseakayaking.com)

Port Douglas

- **Bike N Hike** – half and full-day kayaking trips including visits to Snapper Island; kayak hire available (✆ 07 4099 4000, www.bikenhike.com.au)

Canoeing near Mossman

TOURISM QUEENSLAND

White-Water Rafting

Commercial white-water rafting trips operate in the Barron Gorge near Cairns (grade 3 rapids), on the North Johnstone River near Innisfail (grade 5), on the Russell River also near Innisfail (grade 3-4) and in Tully Gorge near Mission Beach (grade 4). Rapids are graded from 1 to 6, and the higher the number the bigger the thrill. Tully Gorge is considered to be one of the world's most popular white-water rafting venues. Both it and the Barron are raftable all year thanks to the daily release of water from hydroelectric power schemes.

Organised Tours

The following operators provide white-water rafting trips from Cairns, usually in conjunction with other adventure activities such as hot-air ballooning. All do pick-ups in Port Douglas:

- **Foaming Fury** – Barron and Russell rivers (✆ 07 4031 3460, 1800 801 540, www.foamingfury.com.au)
- **Raging Thunder** – Barron and Tully rivers (✆ 07 4030 7990, www.ragingthunder.com.au)
- **R'n'R White Water Rafting** – Tully and North Johnstone rivers (✆ 07 4041 9444, www.raft.com.au)

Expect to pay from around $90/150 ex-Cairns for a rafting trip on the Barron/Tully River. R'n'R does extended seasonal tours on the North Johnstone whereby you fly in by helicopter and raft out. In 2004 they were charging $635/1205 for two/four-day expeditions.

Yachting & Boating

Yachting and boating are popular pastimes along the FNQ coast, particularly as it's so easy to combine them with other great activities like snorkelling, diving and visiting small islands. If you just want to go for a sail but haven't brought your own yacht, the Cairns Yacht Club (✆ 07 4031 2750) and the Port Douglas Yacht Club (✆ 07 4099 4386) both have a 'visitors sailing afternoon' on Wednesdays.

A Recreational Marine Driver Licence is required to operate any recreational boat that is powered by a motor greater than 6hp; is capable of speeds greater than 10 knots; and has a planing or non-displacement hull.

After 1 September 2005 a licence will be required to drive all recreational boats with a motor greater than 6hp.

Remember to keep an eye out for dugong and marine turtles, and be aware of any boating restrictions near islands.

Yacht & Cruiser Hire

You can hire self-drive yachts and motor cruisers, but the choice is limited:

- **Cairns U-Drive Boat Hire** – 6m half-cabin cruisers as well as tinnies (℅ 0408 988 277)
- **Hinchinbrook Rent-a-Yacht** – based at Cardwell with a range of self-drive yachts and motor cruisers for hire. During the high season (Easter and school holiday period, mid-June to 31 October, and mid-December to mid-January) you can cruise the sheltered waters northwards from Hinchinbrook Island to Dunk Island (℅ 07 4066 8007, www.hinchinbrookrentayacht.com.au).
- **Serious Adventures** – based at Cairns with 6.2m centre-console sports boats (℅ 0418 772 751)

Tinnies

The following boat-hire places have outboard-powered tinnies for use in rivers and estuaries. The operators can usually provide fishing tackle and bait as well as directions to where the fish are:

Cairns Area

- **Barron River Tackle** – off the Captain Cook Hwy immediately south of the Barron River Bridge in North Cairns (℅ 07 4058 1437)
- **Cairns Boat Hire & Water Taxi** – at the Marlin Jetty, across from the Reef Fleet Terminal in central Cairns. They're ideally placed for trips on Trinity Inlet (℅ 07 4051 4139, www.cairnsboathire.com.au).
- **Mulgrave River Marina** – at Deeral, south of Gordonvale, handy to the Russell and Mulgrave rivers (℅ 07 4067 5360)
- **Tropical Boat Charters** – in Cairns (℅ 07 4036 2009, tropicalure@picknowl.com.au)

Cooktown Area

- **Bloomfield Boat Hire** – at Ayton on the Bloomfield River (℅ 07 4060 8252, www.bloomfieldcabins.com)

- **Cooktown Cruises** – the Endeavour and Annan rivers await (℅ 07 4069 5712)
- **Getaway Boat Rentals** – in Cooktown (℅ 07 4069 5220)

Innisfail Area

- **Flying Fish Point Boat Hire** – at the Flying Fish Point Van Park (℅ 07 4061 3131, www.ffpvanpark.com.au)
- **Mourilyan Harbour Boat Hire** – ideally placed for trips on the lower Moresby River (℅ 07 4063 2792)

Lake Tinaroo

- **Lake Tinaroo Boat Hire** – at the Lake Tinaroo Holiday Park, Tinaroo (℅ 07 4095 8537, www.tinarooboathire.com)

Mission Beach Area

- **Mission Beach Boat Hire** – at South Mission Beach handy to the Hull River (℅ 0438 688 140)
- **Hull Heads Boat Hire** – close to the Hull River Estuary (℅ 07 4066 9111)

Port Douglas

- **Out 'n' About Boat Hire** – also does fishing charters (℅ 07 4098 5204)
- **Port Douglas Boat Hire** – handy to Dickson Inlet (℅ 07 4099 6277)

TOURISM QUEENSLAND

Kayaking at Lizard Island

Kiteboarding

Kiteboarding (also known as kitesurfing, though there's little surf here) is one of the world's fastest growing sports and appears to have largely taken over from windsurfing in FNQ. Here the kiteboarding season stretches from early May through to late September, when the southeast trade winds are blowing and box jellyfish numbers are at their lowest. The main centres for kiteboarding in this region are Port Douglas and Yorkeys Knob (near Cairns).

The annual **It's Extreme Kite Week**, which takes place at Yorkeys Knob over five days in August, attracts boarders from as far away as Perth and New Zealand.

Lessons

Kiteboarding may appear to be a difficult sport requiring great skill, but according to one instructor all you really need is good coordination. He estimates that the average person with no experience in windsurfing can be up on a board with six to eight hours of tuition. Kiteboarding lessons are provided by:

- **It's Extreme** – Cairns, good source of information on the region's kiteboarding scene, also hires equipment (☎ 07 4051 0344, www.itsextreme.com, 32 Spence St)
- **Traqua** – **Port Douglas**, also hires equipment (☎ 0438 674 584, www.traqua.com).
- **Wind Swell** – Port Douglas (☎ 07 4098 2167, kitesurfportdouglas@bigpond.com).

Aerial Activities

Hang-Gliding & Paragliding

Far North Queensland has an active hang-gliding and paragliding scene, and you can find out what's happening by contacting the Cairns Hang Gliding Club on ☎ 07 4056 1572. Novices can do courses, or take a tandem flight with an accredited instructor. Microlighting is popular too – a microlight is basically a motorised hang-glider.

Scenic Flights & Courses

Tandem hang-gliding flights launch from Rex Lookout, on the Captain Cook Hwy between Palm Cove and Port Douglas. This scenic coastal spot is only usable in southeasterly wind conditions, which is most of the time between early May and late September. Contact the following operators, both of whom charge around $175 for a 30-minute tandem flight:

- **Cairns Hang-Gliding & Micro-Lighting** – tandem hang-gliding flights from Rex Lookout and tandem microlight flights from Port Douglas. Also full-time courses in both hang-gliding and microlighting, which normally take eight to 10 days depending on the wind (☎ 07 4055 3343, 0419 773 309)
- **Tandem Hang Gliding** – hang-gliding flights (☎ 0412 000 797, gregandpatch@yahoo.com.au)

Hot-Air Ballooning

There are three operators, all based in Cairns and all with their take-off points near Mareeba, on the Atherton Tableland. Flights lift off early in the morning to take advantage of the invariably calm conditions at that time. Watching the sun come up over the Tableland is a great way to start the day, particularly when followed by

White-water rafting on the Tully River

Hang-gliding at Rex Lookout

a champagne breakfast. All operators do pick-ups in Cairns and Port Douglas:

- **Champagne Balloon Flights**
  (✆ 07 4058 1688, 1800 677 444,
  www.champagneballoons.com.au)
- **Hot Air Cairns** (✆ 07 4039 2900,
  1800 800 829, www.hotair.com.au)
- **Raging Thunder** (✆ 07 4030 7990,
  www.ragingthunder.com.au)

Hot Air offers a luxury ballooning tour that includes limousine transfers, a 60-minute flight and a gourmet breakfast for $420. The peasants can expect to pay $150/260 for a 30/60-minute flight.

Scenic Flights

The Great Barrier Reef makes a stunning picture when seen from the air, as do the rainforest-clad mountains that line the coast. For a different perspective of these world heritage areas, take a scenic flight with any of the following:

Cairns

- Air Tours Australia (✆ 07 4034 9300,
  1800 246 206, www.airtoursaustralia.com.au)
- Brazakka's Cape York Helicopters
  (✆ 07 4093 0250,
  www.capeyorkhelicopters.com)
- **Down Under Helicopters**
  (✆ 07 4034 9000,
  www.downunderheli.com)
- **Great Barrier Reef Helicopter Group**
  (✆ 07 4035 9669,
  www.gbrhelicopters.com.au)
- **Gulf Line Aviation** – also in Mareeba
  (✆ 1800 458 458)

- **Kestrel Aviation Services**
  (✆ 07 4045 1372,
  www.kestrelaviationservices.com.au)
- **North Qld Air Charter** (✆ 07 4035 9438,
  www.nqaeroclub.com.au)
- **Reef Helicopters** (✆ 07 4034 9420,
  www.reefhelicopters.com.au)
- **Tiger Moth Scenic Flights**
  (✆ 07 4035 9400)

Cape Tribulation
- **Gondwana Aviation** (✆ 07 4098 9054)

Cardwell
- **Cardwell Air Charters** (✆ 07 4066 8468,
  www.oz-e.com.au/cardair)

Cooktown
- **Marine Air Seaplanes** (✆ 07 4069 5915,
  www.marineair.com.au)

Mareeba
- **Air Mareeba** (✆ 07 4092 2181,
  airmareeba@austarnet.com.au)

Parachuting

The following skydiving outfits offer solo and/or tandem jumps, including all necessary tuition:

- **Jump the Beach** – Mission Beach
  (✆ 07 4052 1822, 1800 638 005,
  www.jumpthebeach.com)
- **Paul's Parachuting** – Cairns and Mission Beach (✆ 07 4051 8855, 1800 005 006,
  www.paulsparachuting.com.au)
- **Skydive Cairns** (✆ 07 4031 5466,
  1800 444 568, www.skydivecairns.com.au) ∎

Hot-air ballooning at Mareeba

TOURISM QUEENSLAND

Josephine Falls.

Chapter Four

The Cassowary Coast

The coast between Cardwell and Cairns is marketed as the Cassowary Coast, which rather implies that these amazing birds are quite common here. Sadly, however, the only place you're likely to see a cassowary in the wild these days is in the Mission Beach area.

Cassowaries aside, this stretch of coast and adjoining ranges has many attractions for the outdoors enthusiast. Starting at Cardwell in the south you can visit Hinchinbrook Island and enjoy its abundant natural charms. Just north of town, the road to Blencoe Falls is a must for the more adventurous motorist. It's one of FNQ's most outstanding scenic drives, with one of its most spectacular waterfalls at the end of it. Further north towards Tully, picturesque Murray Falls is easily accessible.

Tully is close to state forests forming part of the Wet Tropics WHA, while Tully Gorge is a major white-water rafting venue. As well, there are a number of fine walks and drives in the forests east of town.

Also east of Tully is a string of superb beaches including Mission Beach, one of the region's more famous stretches of sand. Among other things, you can go diving or snorkelling on a reef trip, take a ferry ride – or paddle a kayak – out to jewel-like Dunk Island, or just laze on the beach wondering what the poor people are doing.

Between Innisfail and Gordonvale, just 24km south of Cairns, the western skyline is dominated by the rugged Francis and Bellenden Ker ranges. Both are within Wooroonooran National Park in the Wet Tropics WHA. Established in 1913, the park includes the state's highest mountains and several readily accessible waterfalls and cascades. Other attractions in the area include Ella Beach, the bird life at Eubenangee Swamp, the Frankland Group of Islands and the view from the summit of Walshs Pyramid.

Cardwell (p122, C3)

On the Bruce Hwy 179km south of Cairns, sleepy Cardwell (pop 1400) is strung out along the narrow channel that separates the mainland from rugged Hinchinbrook Island. It was established in 1864, which makes it FNQ's oldest town. While tourism is an important local industry – thanks largely to the town's proximity to the island – you'll see little or nothing of the kitsch that's so apparent further north at Cairns and Port Douglas.

The QPWS's Cardwell Rainforest & Reef Centre (☏ 07 4066 8601) is at 142 Victoria St.

Cardwell's nature-based attractions include waterfalls, bushwalks, bush camping and scenic drives. You can also take a fishing charter, hire

DENIS O'BYRNE

Rainforest meets bananas near Mission Beach

self-drive yachts, motor cruisers and house-boats or get a bird's-eye view on a scenic flight.

Starting in Cardwell, the 26km **Cardwell Forest Drive** leaves the Bruce Hwy at the BP service station and finishes on the highway about 4km north of town. En route it winds through pine plantations, farmland, open eucalypt forest and rainforest, with detours to lookouts and waterfalls. Its *pièce de résistance* is the **Cardwell Lookouts**, where a 750m walking track links three separate lookout points, one of which offers a stunning view of Hinchinbrook Island. The walk is strenuous to begin with, but the gradients soon become much easier.

Where to Stay

Budget places in Cardwell include:
- Beachcomber Motel & Tourist Park (℡ 07 4066 8550, beachcombercardwell@bigpond.com)
- Cardwell Beach Backpackers (℡ 07 4066 8800, dav2days@hotmail.com)
- Cardwell Van Park (℡ 07 4066 8689)
- Hinchinbrook Hop – tents and van sites (℡ 07 4066 8776)
- Kookaburra Holiday Park (℡ 07 4066 8648, www.kookaburraholidaypark.com.au)
- Marine Hotel – budget rooms (℡ 07 4066 8662)

Hinchinbrook Island
(pp122-123, C3-C4)

Covering around 635 sq km and rising up to 1140m above the sea, rugged Hinchinbrook Island is Australia's largest island national park. It is noted for its mountainous topography and varied habitats, which include mangrove forest, wet tropical rainforest, heath land, beaches, paperbark swamps, eucalypt woodland and, off the coast, fringing coral reefs and seagrass beds.

Information & Permits

Contact the QPWS office in Cardwell (see above) for general information, camping permits and permits to walk the Thorsborne Track.

To avoid disappointment, applications to walk the Track should be made 12 months in advance. Yes, it's that popular! To preserve the wilderness experience, a maximum of 40 persons in groups of no more than six are allowed on the walk at any one time.

What to See & Do

Suitable only for experienced, self-reliant bushwalkers, the 32km **Thorsborne Track** wends its way down the island's east coast between Ramsay Bay in the north and George Point in the south. It's one of Australia's finest coastal walks, and a minimum of three nights and four days should be allowed to complete the full distance.

Fishing on Hinchinbrook Island

Cassowary Coast

The Hinchinbrook Island Resort at Cape Richards (☎ 07 4066 8725) offers guided walks and snorkelling trips, and you can hire fishing tackle and canoes. Day-trippers are welcome.

At **Scraggy Point**, in the island's northwestern corner, you can see about 2ha of rock enclosures that were built by Aboriginal people to act as fish traps. Nearby is a large midden made up of the detritus of innumerable seafood meals.

Getting There

Water taxis operating out of Cardwell provide casual transport to the island. Check with the information centre for current operators.

Hinchinbrook Island Ferries (☎ 07 4066 8270, www.hinchinbrookferries.com.au) operates daily between Cardwell and the Hinchinbrook Island Resort from April to the end of October, and less often at other times. The day trip costs $85 and hiker/camper drop-off/pick-up costs $59 one-way.

Where to Stay

Apart from the Hinchinbrook Island Resort (☎ 07 4066 8585, www.hinchinbrookresort.com.au), there are two QPWS camping areas in the north, at Scraggy Point and Macushla Bay just southwest of Cape Richards (☎ 13 13 04).

Edmund Kennedy National Park (p122, B2-B3)

If you're staying overnight in Cardwell, the beachfront picnic area in the Edmund Kennedy National Park, 9km north of town, is a nice place to have breakfast. If it's a calm morning you may be lucky enough to spot a dugong – a nearby sign explains what to look for. There are great views from the beach of the chain of islands that include Hinchinbrook and Dunk.

The park contains remnants of the lowland coastal rainforest and melaleuca swamps that once covered the coastal plains between Cardwell and the Daintree. These vegetation communities caused huge problems for the ill-fated explorer Edmund Kennedy, who was forced to fight his way through the dense bush while searching for a route through the ranges.

Today you can get a feel for what Kennedy endured by taking either or both of the walking tracks that lead north from the picnic area. The 1.3km **Wreck Creek Track** forms part of the 3.5km **Mangrove Circuit**, which ends at the access road. Wreck Creek (about 1.5km north of the picnic area) and Meunga Creek (the same distance south) are both inhabited by saltwater crocodiles. Don't forget the sand-fly repellent.

In the wet season check road conditions with the information centre in town. Note that the road is unsuitable for caravans regardless of the season.

Murray Falls (p122, B2)

Murray Falls, in state forest at the foot of the Kirrama Range about halfway between Cardwell and Tully, is generally considered to be one of North Queensland's prettiest waterfalls. On a hot day its deep plunge pool brings swimming to mind. Sadly, however, this activity is officially banned on the grounds that it's too dangerous. The falls can be viewed from **lookouts** along a 150m boardwalk, and at the end of a 900m rainforest track. The latter, which is rocky in parts, has signs relating the traditional Aboriginal use of various plants.

The QPWS camping area (☎ 13 13 04) is suitable for tents and caravans. Firewood is usually provided – the wood heap is on your right as you enter the park.

ROB VAN DRIESUM

Murray Falls – a modest drop but very pretty

Cassowary Coast

The Road to Blencoe Falls (p122, B2-B1)

The narrow, unsealed road that links the tiny township of Kennedy, on the Bruce Hwy 10km north of Cardwell, to Blencoe Falls in the **Lumholtz National Park**, is one of North Queensland's most interesting bush drives. Much of this 71km route was constructed in the early 1930s to allow access to the rainforest for logging. Just surveying it must have been an adventure, to say the least.

Leaving the Bruce Hwy at the Kennedy Store, you take Kennedy Creek Rd through banana plantations and cane fields to an intersection at 6.6km, where you turn right onto Kirrama Rd. About 2km later the road enters the WHA and begins to climb. For the next 20km, wet tropical rainforest crowds the road which has many tight bends as it zigzags up the mountainside. The experience is akin to driving through a long, corkscrewing, green tunnel.

Blencoe Falls is still an impressive sight in the dry season

ROB VAN DRIESUM

After about 8.5km you arrive at **Tucker's Lookout**, 17km from Kennedy. This vantage point offers a superb vista over a flat mosaic of farmland in the Kennedy Valley to the rugged Cardwell Range and Hinchinbrook Island. The view from the **Murray Valley Lookout**, 2.5km further on, is much more restricted, but still worth stopping for.

The next major stop is **Society Flat**, about 31km from Kennedy. For many years this was the site of a logging community, but today any evidence of its existence (apart from tree stumps) is well hidden by the dense vegetation. An easy 700m **circuit walk** reveals some huge kauris and rose gums that escaped the woodsman's axe. The rainforest begins to cut out past here, and by the time you reach the signposted turn-off to Ravenshoe, at 46km, you're in open eucalypt forest with a grassy understorey. The grid 100m further on marks the end of

the WHA and the start of cattle country.

The final 20km to the **Blencoe Creek Bridge** is a winding, roller-coaster ride that will test nervous stomachs. There are good bush campsites by running water on either side of the bridge. Get a camping permit from the QPWS office in Cardwell, and while you're at it ask about access to the foot of **Blencoe Falls**.

Continuing 900m past the bridge you come to a minor road on the left that leads about 4.5km to the best viewing point. From here there's a reasonably unimpeded view of Blencoe Creek as it plunges in a series of drops into the mighty **Herbert Gorge**. The first drop is 91m – an inspiring sight in the dry season, and absolutely awesome during the Wet. A short walking track leads to another viewing point.

Leaving the falls you can either return to Kennedy or continue 113km through cattle country along the main track to Mount Garnet, a small township on the Kennedy Hwy west of Ravenshoe. Another option is the 4WD track to Lake Koombooloomba – head back towards Kennedy and turn left onto the road to Ravenshoe. You need a QPWS "permit to traverse" for this route.

The Kennedy Store has a leaflet that gives a brief route description and includes a fairly detailed mud map of the Blencoe Falls area. Allow a full day to do the return drive including stops for lunch, the Society Flat walk, and the various lookouts. Plan to stay overnight if you want to take the long scramble down into the gorge.

Finally, this route is inaccessible to conventional vehicles in wet conditions. As far as hazards go, by far the worst is oncoming traffic – approach blind corners with care. The road is most definitely *not* suitable for caravans.

Tully & Surrounds (p122, A2)

Tully (pop 3500), off the Bruce Hwy 135km from Cairns, was established as a sugar-milling centre in the 1920s and doesn't appear to have changed much since then. Looming above the town on its western side is the rugged, rainforest-clad **Walter Hill Range**, while a grimy sugar mill dominates the east. Tully is Australia's second-wettest town (after Babinda) and holds the record for the highest rainfall in one year (7900mm).

The Tully Visitor & Heritage Centre (✆ 07 4068 2299, www.csc.qld.gov.au) is on the Bruce Hwy near the turn-off to town.

What to See & Do

Apart from guided tours of the sugar mill there's not a lot to do in Tully itself. One thing worth stopping for – but only on a clear day – is a hike to the summit of **Mt Tyson** (687m). The walk is steep and strenuous, with some scrambling involved, but the views are magnificent. Allow at least three hours for the return walk. To get there, drive up the main street to the T-junction and turn left onto Brannigan St – the walk starts at the end of the street. Visitor centre staff ask that you record your intentions on the whiteboard outside the ambulance station, which you pass en route to Brannigan St.

Seven km north of town, **Alligators Nest** is a popular swimming hole in a state forest park. Despite the name there are no lurking crocodiles.

Tully is handy to two of FNQ's major attractions – Mission Beach and Tully Gorge. White-water rafting is popular in the gorge, and skydiving tours over the beach operate from the airport. Tully is also a jumping-off point for hikers heading for the high-altitude walking tracks in the Misty Mountains between here and Ravenshoe (see boxed text p87).

Tully Gorge (p122, A2-A1; p118, E1)

Heading out of town on Tully Gorge Rd you enter World Heritage rainforest at 36km and come to the **Tully River Bridge** 4km further on. On the right, and immediately before the bridge, the 'H' Track heads off to the Misty Mountains' Cochable Creek track head.

About 2.5km past the bridge, the **Frank Roberts Lookout** provides a great view of the river and gorge. Just 500m further on, the **Tully Gorge National Park** has a large swimming hole under a tall, rainforest-clad cliff, and pleasant picnic and camping areas. There's also the Butterfly Walk, a 400m rainforest circuit track with interpretive signs that tell you about local butterflies.

Continuing up the gorge the road passes small parking areas from which you can access the river to watch the daily procession of adrenaline-crazed rafters as they negotiate the rapids. Check the times with the visitor centre in Tully. The road ends at the Kareeya Hydroelectric Power Station at the foot of Tully Falls.

Tenacious root system, Murray Falls

Mangrove forest, Edmund Kennedy National Park

Cassowary Coast

Tully Heads (p122, B3)

Turning off the highway 6km south of Tully, the Tully Hull Rd provides access to the little holiday settlements of Hull Heads and Tully Heads. These are at the northern and southern ends respectively of stunning **Googarra Beach**, which has views of the Family Islands about 10km offshore. **Bedarra Island**, due east of Hull Heads, is the setting for an exclusive resort. The island is privately owned and entry is restricted.

You can hire outboard-powered tinnies (✆ 07 4066 9888) in Hull Heads for trips on the Hull River estuary.

Where to Stay

There are two caravan parks in the area:
• Googarra Beach Caravan Park (✆ 07 4066 9352)
• Bedarra View Caravan Park (✆ 07 4066 9260)

Mission Beach (p122, A3)

Mission Beach is actually made up of four separate communities (South Mission Beach, Wongaling Beach, Mission Beach and Bingil Bay) scattered along 14km of palm-fringed coastline. This is one of FNQ's favourite holiday playgrounds, with many activities and nature-based attractions to tempt the visitor. The Great Barrier Reef is an hour away by fast catamaran, while Dunk Island – home of one of Queensland's best-known resorts – is just 5km offshore.

Information

The Mission Beach Visitor Information Centre (✆ 07 4068 7099, www.missionbeachtourism.com) is on Porter Promenade in Mission Beach. The Wet Tropics Environment Centre (✆ 07 4068 7179) is in the same complex.

Improvised shelter, Mission Beach

What to See & Do

There are plenty of outdoor and nature-based activities in and around Mission Beach and nearby Dunk Island. For the more adventurous visitor there's parachuting with Jump the Beach (✆ 1800 638 005) and Paul's Parachuting (✆ 1800 005 006), white-water rafting with Raging Thunder (✆ 07 4068 8580) and R'n'R (✆ 07 4051 7777) and sea-kayaking trips (short and extended) with Coral Sea Kayaking (✆ 07 4068 9154).

Day trips to the Reef are available with QuickCat Cruises (✆ 07 4068 7289), Calypso Dive (✆ 07 4068 8432) and Blue Thunder Cruises (✆ 07 4068 7211). Calypso Dive also offers diving courses. Mission Beach Boat Hire (✆ 0438 688 140) at South Mission Beach rents catamarans and outboard-powered tinnies, while Dunk Island Ferry & Cruises (✆ 07 4068 7211) does cruises to Dunk and Bedarra islands.

Other activities include cruises on the Hull River, fishing charters, swimming, bushwalking, bird-watching and lazing about admiring the view of beautiful Dunk Island. A couple of good spots for shore fishing are the boat ramp and jetty at Clump Point, where there's a chance of catching mackerel, barramundi, shark, trevally, queenfish, coral trout and mud crabs.

Bushwalks

The area around 'town' has a good variety of walks. For a pleasant stroll along the foreshore try the **Cutten Brothers Walk** and the **Ulysses Walk**. These gravel paths – one is an extension of the other – link the Clump Point jetty to the Village Green at The Hub shopping centre, in Mission Beach. Allow 45 minutes one way.

For something a little more strenuous there's the **Kennedy Track**, a 7km return coastal walk that's reputed to be one of the best of its genre in North Queensland. The track starts at the boat ramp at the southern end of South Mission Beach and ends at **Kennedy Bay**, where the explorer Edmund Kennedy began his ill-fated journey to Cape York in 1848. From here you can continue a further 2km along the beach to the **Hull River Mouth**, making a total distance of 11km. There's plenty of variety along this excellent walk – stunning island views, rainforest, mangroves, huge calophyllum trees, deserted beaches, rocky bluffs and much more.

The 4km **Bicton Hill Circuit** in Clump Mountain National Park is another good walk. This one starts on the coast road between Mission Beach and Bingil Bay, with the track head being about 2km from the Clump Point jetty. The track is moderately steep, but the rainforest and some great views make the effort worthwhile.

The **Tam O'Shanter State Forest** between the Bruce Hwy and Mission Beach contains a tract of lowland rainforest that forms one of FNQ's last strongholds of the endangered cassowary. Good spots to see these elusive birds are the Licuala State Forest Park on Tully-Mission Beach Rd and the Lacey Creek State Forest Park, on El Arish-Mission Beach Rd. Each has an easy and enjoyable 1.2km interpretive circuit walk, and a 7km path links the two.

Where to Stay

The Mission Beach area has plenty of up-market accommodation. Following are some of the budget places:

South Mission Beach

- Beachcomber Coconut Village
  (☎ 07 4068 8129, www.big4.com.au)

- Dunk Island View Van Park
  (☎ 07 4068 8248,
  www.dunkislandviewcp.bizland.com)
- Tropical Hibiscus Caravan Park
  (☎ 07 4068 8138,
  tropicalhibiscuscaravanpark.com)

Wongaling Beach

- Mission Beach Backpackers Lodge
  (☎ 07 4068 8317,
  www.missionbeachbackpacker.com)

Mission Beach

- Beach Shack Backpacker Resort
  (☎ 1800 333 115,
  www.misionbeachshack.com)
- Hideaway Holiday Village (☎ 07 4068 7104,
  hideaway@austarnet.com.au)
- Mission Beach Caravan Park (☎ 07 4068 7104)
- Mission Beach Retreat (☎ 07 4088 6229,
  www.missionbeachretreat.com.au)

Bingil Bay

- Bingil Bay Backpackers Resort
  (☎ 07 4068 7208, www.nomadsworld.com)
- Sanctuary Retreat (☎ 07 4088 6064,
  www.sanctuaryretreat.com.au)
- Treehouse YHA Hostel (☎ 07 4068 7137)

Fan palms in the Licuala State Forest Park

Cassowaries inhabit the forests around Mission Beach, but their numbers have declined dramatically and few visitors are lucky enough to see them in the wild

Cassowary Coast

Dunk Island (p122, A3)

Beautiful Dunk Island is a high continental island, most of which is covered by rainforest and eucalypt forest. About three-quarters of its total area of 970ha is national park, the remainder being privately owned. While there are no restrictions on visiting the national park, day-trippers need a pass to make use of the resort's facilities. Passes cost $40 (*not* inclusive of transport) and are available at the resort's water sports shop.

Good things on offer on the island include water sports such as snorkelling on the fringing reef, swimming, kayaking and sailing (catamarans and sailboards can be hired at the resort), beach walks, bushwalks and bird-watching (over 100 species).

The national park has 13km of walking tracks with routes ranging from 15 minutes to three hours. It takes about two hours to do the return walk from the jetty to the top of **Mt Kootaloo** (271m), the island's highest point. From here you get a marvellous view of the other islands in the Family Group.

Getting There

The venerable MV *Lawrence Kavanagh*, operated by Dunk Island Ferry & Cruises (℃ 07 4068 7211, www.dunkferry.com.au), departs twice daily from the Clump Point jetty charging $22 return.

Dunk Island Water Taxi (℃ 07 4068 8310) departs five times daily from Wongaling Beach during the tourist season, charging $15 one-way. They'll also take you to other members of the Family Group, such as Wheeler and Coombe islands.

QuickCat Cruises does day trips to Dunk Island.

Where to Stay

The Dunk Island Resort (℃ 07 4068 8199, www.dunkislandresort.com) has a variety of room styles costing from $250 twin-share. A resort-operated QPWS camping area is near the jetty. Bookings are essential.

Old Bruce Highway (p118, D2)

About 25km north of Tully you come to the Silkwood-Japoon Rd, the old Bruce Highway. This pleasant, scenic back road makes an interesting alternative to the 'new' highway to Innisfail. Apart from the views, you'll pass through a string of quaint little sugar towns, all with photographic appeal.

One of these townships is Mena Creek, where the main attraction is **Paronella Park** (℃ 07 4065 3225, www.paronellapark.com.au). This fascinating Spanish-style castle and 'pleasure garden' were constructed in this most un-Iberian spot by Spanish expats Jose & Margarita Paronella in the 1930s. Floods,

TOURISM QUEENSLAND

Dunk Island

Cassowary Coast

cyclones and fire have taken their toll. Even so, it's easy to spend an hour wandering about the gardens and various structures while marvelling at the seemingly boundless dedication and energy of their creators. Entry costs $22 including the Aboriginal-guided **bush tucker walk**.

Mena Creek Rd turns off at the pub to provide access to the Misty Mountains walks.

Innisfail (p118, D3)

On the Bruce Hwy 83km south of Cairns, Innisfail (pop 9000) is a busy service centre where tourism is pretty much a poor cousin to sugar and bananas. The town was largely rebuilt in the 1920s after being blown away by a cyclone, and this has left an unusually rich legacy of **Art Deco** architecture. Art Deco was a style period between the two world wars, when concrete first began to be widely used as a construction medium for commercial and public buildings.

The Innisfail Information Centre (℡ 07 4061 7422, www.jsc.qld.gov.au) is on the Bruce Hwy at the Tully end of town.

What to See & Do

Anyone with even a passing interest in architecture should stop and do one of the entertaining **Art Deco walking tours** (℡ 07 4061 9008) that depart daily from the Shire Hall on Rankin St. Also in town, the 50ha **Warrina Lakes** complex features freshwater lagoons, rainforest walks, a botanic garden with many local species, a bush tucker garden and recreation areas.

The **Johnstone River** flows through town and there are many good fishing spots along its banks. Barramundi (in season), mangrove jack, bream and trevally are the main catches.

Heading east from town on Flying Fish Point Rd you pass the **Johnstone River Crocodile Farm**, which has tours daily. The farm runs a cassowary-breeding program aimed at increasing the wild population of these birds.

Flying Fish Point, 7km from Innisfail, is a quiet holiday community near the mouth of the Johnstone River. Outboard-powered tinnies can be hired from the caravan park (℡ 07 4061 3131, www.ffpvanpark.com.au) for fishing trips on the river.

Paronella Park, a Spanish couple's dream come true

Etty Bay

South Wooroonooran

(p118, D2-D1)

The Palmerston Hwy between Innisfail and Millaa Millaa passes through some wonderfully scenic country including Wet Tropics rainforest at the southern end of Wooroonooran National Park. Within the latter are several attractions that are definitely worth attention.

Heading west, the first of these is found about 500m inside the park boundary. This is **Crawfords Lookout**, from where a 1.6km walking track zigzags down the slope to a lookout with a spectacular view of the North Johnstone River. Buttressed trees are a feature of this walk, which has a steep detour to the river.

About 2km further on is the track head for short walks to **Tchupala Falls** (400m) and **Wallicher Falls** (800m), followed by the K-Tree Rd turn-off to the **South Johnstone Campsite** (12.8km) and the **Misty Mountains** walks (p87). This minor forest road features huge king ferns – also known as angiopteris ferns, this ancient species has the largest fronds of any fern in the world.

Back on the highway it's another 1.6km to the delightful **Goolagan Creek** picnic area. The **Henrietta Creek Campsite**, a beaut spot for a rainforest camping experience, is about 700m further on. A walking track links the campground to Goolagan Creek, and if you're quiet you may see musky rat kangaroos and platypuses. There's also the 7.2km **Nandroya Falls Circuit**, which features two spectacular waterfalls, steep topography and some deep pools to cool off in. Local bushwalkers suggest doing this walk in an anticlockwise direction. Allow three to four hours to complete the full circuit.

For information on these walks, contact the rangers on ☎ 07 4064 5115.

Just to the north of here is **Ella Bay National Park** and its beautiful, unspoilt beach – a long, sweeping crescent of golden sand with rainforest coming down to the high-water mark. This is a great venue for a remote beach walk, and except on weekends you'll probably have the place to yourself. The unsealed access 'road' stops at a locked gate 3.5km from the edge of town – to find the start, simply follow the signs through town.

There are several **bush campsites** with no facilities by the beach in Ella Bay National Park. You'll find them in the final 400m before the locked gate.

Southeast of Innisfail is **Etty Bay** and yet another stunning beach. Etty Bay is off the Mourilyan Harbour Rd, which intersects the Bruce Hwy 6km south of town. There's a caravan park here also (☎ 07 4063 2314).

North from Innisfail

Heading out of Innisfail on the Bruce Hwy towards Cairns you soon come to an intersection with the **Palmerston Hwy**. The latter heads west for 60km to Millaa Millaa, passing walking tracks and camping and picnic areas at the southern end of Wooroonooran National Park. See the boxed text.

Continuing northwards on the Bruce Hwy the first major stop is **Josephine Falls** (p118, C2), a major scenic attraction at the foot of the Bellenden Ker Range. The 600m sealed path to the falls leads through a fine example of complex mesophyll vine forest, and a sign en route reveals that the creek is home to the endangered Australian lace-lid frog. While you're unlikely to see a lace-lid frog, scrub turkeys scratching in the leaf litter are a common sight.

The picnic area at Josephine Falls is the main starting point for treks to the summit of

King fern along K-Tree Rd, Misty Mountains

ROB VAN DRIESUM

Mt Bartle Frere (1622m) (p118, C2), Queensland's highest point. Allow at least 12 hours to complete the strenuous 15km return walk, or to do the one-way trek over the top to the Gourka Rd track head. Alternatively, the 10km return hike from the falls to **Broken Nose** (962m) takes a mere eight hours! Note that the range is covered in cloud eight days out of 10 and receives rain 250 days in a year on average. Be prepared for a sudden onset of cold, wet weather.

For advice and information on these walks, contact the rangers at Mirriwinni on ☏ 07 4067 6304. If starting your Bartle Frere trek from the west, talk to the rangers at Lake Eacham on ☏ 07 4095 3768 – they can provide directions for vehicle access to the track head. Details on the various walking options are found in the QPWS's excellent brochure **Mt Bartle Frere Trail**.

Back on the Bruce Hwy, the turn-off to Bramston Beach soon appears on the right. Turn here and follow the signs to **Eubenangee Swamp** (p118, C2), one of FNQ's prime birding spots. An easy 1500m circuit walk takes you through lowland rainforest along the Alice River to a grassy hilltop that overlooks the swamp. You'll need powerful binoculars or a telescope to see the birds, which tend to congregate some distance from the lookout.

Bramston Beach (p118, C3) is another small holiday centre with stunning coastal scenery. From the car park at the end of the main road you look northwards along a pristine curve of sand to the forested hills of **Russell River National Park** (p118, C2), with the Frankland Group of Islands and Fitzroy Island clearly visible in the distance. There are two caravan parks here, or you can camp in the national park. To get to the latter, turn left on Sassafras St and follow the main track for 6km to the park entry point. Several sites are scattered along the beach in the 1.5km between here and the end of the track.

Heading northwards on the Bruce Hwy once more, you come to the attractive little township of **Babinda** (p118, C2), about 7km past Bramston Beach Rd. Its main attraction is **The Boulders**, a council reserve on Babinda Creek 6.5km west of town. Here you'll find a swimming hole, rainforest walking tracks and some dramatic scenery along the boulder-strewn creek – particularly when it's in flood. On the edge of the forest is a free campground with

Behana Gorge

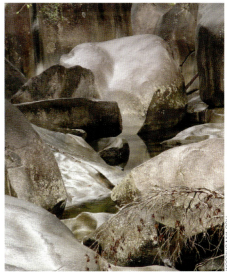
The Boulders at Babinda

Swimming hole at the Boulders

Cassowary Coast

five sites. Within the reserve, the 850m Jungle Circuit takes you on a pleasant stroll through lowland rainforest, while the 1.2km Devil's Pool Walk leads along the creek to a gorge lookout. Both walks are graded easy, but stay away from the granite boulders which are crumbly and slippery.

The Boulders marks the start of the 19km **Goldfield Track** across the Bellenden Ker Range to the Goldsborough Valley Forest Reserve. Gold prospectors first opened up this route, which crosses a saddle between Mt Bartle Frere and Mt Bellenden Ker, during a minor rush in the 1930s. The walk is strenuous, but exhilarating, and takes seven or eight hours to complete. Huge king ferns are a feature.

About 13km north of Babinda is the hamlet of **Deeral** (p118, B2), where you can hire outboard-powered tinnies for fishing trips on the Mulgrave and Russell rivers. Deeral is where you catch the boat to the Frankland Group. **Fishery Falls**, 6km further on, is close to some small but pretty cascades in the rainforest. To get there, turn left immediately past the caravan park.

The final waterfall in this series is in **Behana Gorge** (p118, B2), the turn-off to which is 9km north of Fishery Falls. It's 4.5km from the highway to a locked gate, after which you walk (or jog, or cycle) along a mainly straight, concreted road for the final 3km to **Clamshell Falls**. The gorge scenery is attractive and there are deep, crystal-clear pools to cool off in.

The dominant landmark in this part of the world is the almost perfectly cone-shaped mass of **Walshs Pyramid** (922m) (p118, B2), at the northern ends of the Bellenden Ker Range and Wooroonooran National Park. The parking area is on Moss Rd and from there it's a long, steep trek to the summit, where the reward (on a clear day) is magnificent views to all points of the compass. Each year in August a foot race is held from Gordonvale to the summit, and back again. The race record is around 80 minutes, which will elicit a gasp of admiration when you look at the course. It takes the average visitor nearly twice that just to get to the summit – and the car park is a lot closer than Gordonvale.

Goldsborough Valley (p118, B2)

From Moss Rd it's 1.8km to the junction of the Bruce and Gillies highways, where you either continue straight ahead to Cairns (24km) or turn left to the Atherton Tableland and the **Goldsborough Valley Forest Reserve**. To reach the latter, which adjoins Wooroonooran National Park, turn left at about 6km from the intersection and follow the narrow winding road along the Mulgrave River for 12km to the QPWS camping area. This is the terminus for the Goldfield Track from The Boulders. If you're planning on starting the trek here, the 1.7km return walk through beautiful rainforest to **Kearneys Falls** makes a delicious entrée. Swimming and canoeing in the Mulgrave River are popular activities here. ∎

Lazing in the Goldsborough Valley Forest Reserve

Chapter Five

Cairns & Surrounds

Almost surrounded by the steep, forested mountains of the Great Dividing Range, Cairns is the international gateway for visits to the surrounding World Heritage Areas and the Atherton Tableland. An estimated two million holiday-makers – many from Japan – visit the town each year and venture forth from there.

Cairns (p128; p118, A2)

Cairns (which the locals pronounce almost like "cans") has a population of around 120,000 and is Queensland's fourth-largest town after Brisbane, Toowoomba and Townsville. As well as being a major regional centre and port, it's an important tourist destination – second only to Sydney among visitors from overseas.

The Great Barrier Reef is the major attraction and an impressive fleet of boats waits to take you there (see Fishing pp41-45 and Diving & Snorkelling pp45-49). As well, many options are centred on the river and rainforest environments including trail rides, mountain-bike rides and white-water rafting. You can take to the air in a hang-glider, hot-air balloon or scenic flight, or dangle from a parachute. Alternatively, keep your feet on the ground on the many jungle walking tracks near Cairns.

From Cairns it's less than an hour by either car or boat to several regional highlights including Kuranda, Port Douglas, Green and Fitzroy islands, and the Bellenden Ker Range.

Mt Whitfield Conservation Park

Overlooking the Cairns airport on the northern side of town, Mt Whitfield is a 300ha island of native bush surrounded by housing and industrial developments. The entrance is on MacDonnell St just off Collins Ave in the suburb of Edge Hill. For information, contact the Flecker Botanic Gardens on ℂ 07 4044 3398.

The park's often precipitous slopes were home to an isolated population of cassowaries until the late 1990s, when dogs killed the last one. Yet despite the unwelcome attentions of man's best friend, the scrub turkeys and scrub fowls seem to be thriving. Both species are often seen scratching around on the forest floor along the walking tracks that lead up to Mt Whitfield (360m) and Lumley Hill (325m).

TOURISM QUEENSLAND

Cairns

There are two linked rainforest walks. The 1.5km **Red Arrow Circuit**, which is well made but steep, starts at the car park and leads to a lookout point that offers views over the central business district and airport. Continue past here and you come to the 5.5km **Blue Arrow Circuit** – walk carefully as tangled tree roots soon replace the steps! This testing route includes the aforementioned hills and is popular with weekend joggers. Allow one hour for the red circuit and at least five hours to do them both.

Flecker Botanic Gardens

The entrance to this excellent facility is on Collins Ave just a stone's throw from Mt Whitfield Conservation Park. Here you'll find displays of plants from the world's tropical equatorial zone – the collections of heliconias, gingers, backscratcher ginger and palms are particularly noteworthy. The **Centenary Lakes** have both fresh and saltwater habitats, which makes them of interest to bird-watchers too. Also featured is **Australia's Gondwanan Heritage**, a fascinating display devoted to the development of Australia's wet tropics flora. Another highlight is a beautiful remnant of the lowland swamp forest that covered much of the Cairns Plain prior to White settlement. You can explore it on a 400m boardwalk.

The gardens are open daily and there's a licensed café on the premises. Guided tours ($10) operate on weekdays (℡ 07 4044 3398).

Mangrove Walks

Take Airport Ave to the Cairns airport and you'll pass the car park for the **Jack Barnes Bicentennial Mangrove Boardwalks** on your right. There are two elevated walkways, both about 1km in length and with very informative signage that provides an insight into the fascinating world of a mangrove forest. You'll come away with a heightened appreciation of why these habitats must be protected, not thoughtlessly destroyed to make way for 'lifestyle' coastal developments. On the down side, mangroves are prime breeding areas for sand flies and this area is no exception. Don't forget the insect repellent.

Barron Gorge National Park
(p118, A1; p114, E1)

The Barron River rises on the Atherton Tableland, and by the time it reaches the coast just north of the Cairns airport it has become a substantial stream. En route the river has carved out the mighty **Barron Gorge**, a wild and rugged place of sheer cliffs and steep, forested slopes. It's the major topographic feature of the 2820ha Barron Gorge National Park, which forms part of the Wet Tropics WHA. The park includes the full length of the gorge from Kuranda to its downstream end on the northern fringes of Cairns. Its most famous highlight, **Barron Falls**, can be viewed from lookouts near Kuranda.

Cairns torch ginger, commonly known as backscratcher ginger

Lake Placid

The best way to appreciate the park is to walk, and the good news is that a network of walking tracks links Kuranda with Cairns and the **Speewah Campground** (in the park's southwest corner). They include the **Douglas** and **Smith tracks**, both of which wend their way between track heads at Speewah and Stony Creek Rd, off Kamerunga Rd in suburban Kamerunga. Originally used over thousands of years by Aboriginal people travelling to and from the coastal lowlands, these two tracks formed part of the first packhorse routes from Cairns to the Hodgkinson River Goldfield in the 1870s. They are recommended for experienced walkers only.

If you've only got an hour or so, the 750m **Djing-wu Track**, which links the Speewah track head to the Douglas and Smith tracks, is a delightful rainforest walk.

Speewah is accessed by car off the Kennedy Hwy west of Kuranda. It's about 8km from Kuranda to the well-signposted turn-off, from where it's another 6km via Speewah Rd and Stony Creek Rd to the campground.

Another park drawcard, **Lake Placid** is an attractive swimming spot at the gorge's bottom end in Caravonica (a suburb adjoining Kamerunga, a northwestern outer suburb of Cairns). There are no deadly jellyfish here, so this natural ponding area is an extremely popular alternative to the coast during the stinger season. Facilities include picnic furniture and a kiosk and bar. To get there, take Lake Placid Drive off Kamerunga Drive.

Lake Placid is the terminus for the commercial **white-water rafting trips** that depart from the Barron Gorge hydroelectric power station. The station becomes operational for three hours or so in the morning, releasing sufficient water to make rafting possible. At other times during the dry season the river's flow is scarcely enough to carry a leaf downstream.

Kuranda (p114, E1)

At the northern end of the Atherton Tableland, Kuranda – the so-called "Village in the Rainforest" – is off the Kennedy Hwy just 25km by road from the centre of Cairns. Thanks to its elevated position on top of the Kuranda Range, it has long been a summer refuge from the stifling heat and humidity of the lowlands. Today it's one of the region's most popular tourist attractions. Judging by the number of cafés, arts & crafts galleries, souvenir outlets and the like, shopping has become the major lure for day-trippers.

The Kuranda Visitor Information Centre (℡ 07 4093 9311, www.kuranda.org) is on Therwine St just a short walk from the markets.

DENIS O'BYRNE

A reflective moment in Barron Gorge

TOURISM QUEENSLAND

Barron Falls overflowing at the height of the wet season

What to See & Do

Kuranda is an attractive place to visit but there isn't a lot on offer in the way of outdoor activities – apart from strolling (or fighting your way) between the shops. Ask at the visitor centre for a map of the various walks in and around Kuranda. You can also do a cruise on the Barron River above the falls with Kuranda Rainforest Tours (☏ 07 4093 7476).

Most visitors want to see **Barron Falls**, but the river has been harnessed for hydroelectric power generation so they aren't terribly exciting most of the time. It's a different story at the height of the wet season, however, when they present an awesome spectacle. The falls can be viewed from a **lookout** at the end of Barron Falls Rd, 3km from Kuranda. From here a partially elevated walkway winds down through beautiful rainforest for 200m to end at another lookout, this one beside the railway. The latter is the best vantage point for photographs.

A couple of nature-based attractions worth visiting in Kuranda itself are **Bird World** and the **Australian Butterfly Sanctuary**, both of which are accessible through the Heritage Markets. Bird World features a huge walk-through aviary containing numerous native and exotic birds, including a cassowary. The Butterfly Sanctuary displays a number of local species of these gorgeous insects – including the birdwing and Ulysses butterflies – in a well-presented, walk-through rainforest setting. The entry fee to both places is around $12.

Getting There

Opened in 1891, the railway between Cairns and Kuranda includes 15 tunnels, dozens of bridges and 93 bends on its run through the Barron Gorge. Today, trains operated by the Kuranda Scenic Railway (☏ 07 4036 9249, www.ksr.com.au) provide daily return services between the two centres, charging $35/50 for single/return tickets.

For something entirely different, the Skyrail Rainforest Cableway (☏ 07 4038 1555, www.skyrail.com.au) provides a bird's-eye view of the Barron Gorge as it travels back and forth above the rainforest between Cairns and Kuranda. A ticket costs $35/50 single/return.

Kuranda Markets

Elevated walkway to Barron Falls lookout

The Kuranda Scenic Railway winds its way up the range from Cairns

Cairns & Surrounds

The Black Mountain Road (p114, E1-D1; p113, D7-D6)

Connecting Kuranda and Julatten, the 48km Black Mountain Rd along the MacAlister Range provides an adventurous alternative to the Captain Cook Hwy. For the most part this unsealed route winds through World Heritage rainforest in the Kuranda State Forest. A QPWS "permit to traverse" is required between Flaggy Creek and the Bump Track.

Starting at the Kuranda end, Black Mountain Rd leaves the Kennedy Hwy just before the Barron River Bridge. The 18km to Flaggy Creek is a formed gravel road passing through pine plantations and rainforest. At the bridge the road deteriorates into a rough and narrow 4WD track over which hang lawyer vines with their nasty hooked tendrils – keep your arms inside the vehicle, please. Other hazards include fallen trees and bog holes after rain, but in dry conditions the driving is generally easy. The grades are relatively gentle, making this a good option for mountain-bike riders looking for an easy ride.

With 7km to go, you pass the Bump Track and suddenly the road improves dramatically. From here it's formed gravel through forest and farmland to the intersection with Eulema Creek Rd, where you turn either left to Julatten and Mount Molloy, or right to Mossman.

The Black Mountain Rd is rough in places but no problem for mountain bikers

The Skyrail Rainforest Cableway to/from Kuranda, great in combination with the Kuranda Railway – take one up and the other down

DENIS O'BYRNE

Cairns Lagoon, the only place where you can swim on the Cairns waterfront

Allow some time to visit the Tjapukai Aboriginal Cultural Park (📞 07 4042 9999, www.tjapukai.com.au), which is located beside the Cairns terminus.

Visitors who wish to travel one way on the train and the other in a gondola can purchase a ticket for $70 – add $7 for the shuttle bus between the cableway and railway terminuses which are some distance apart in Cairns.

Where to Stay

There is quite a bit of accommodation in and around Kuranda, including these budget places:

- Kuranda Backpackers Hostel
  (📞 07 4093 7355,
  www.kurandabackpackershostel.com)
- Kuranda Rainforest Park
  (📞 07 4093 7316,
  info@kurandarainforestpark.com.au)

Crystal Cascades (p118, A1)

Located within the WHA, the aptly named Crystal Cascades on **Freshwater Creek** include several pools that are popular swimming spots in the stinger season. Take care on the slippery rocks. The pools are accessed from a 1.2km sealed pathway that follows the creek into a narrow gorge clothed in magnificent rainforest.

Another spot worth mentioning is a little waterfall and plunge pool that are just a few minutes' walk along a side creek from the car park's far end. This gem is reserved for those few visitors who are 'in the know'. The route, which isn't signposted, is a goat track with many exposed tree roots. Tread carefully!

The cascades are in state forest at the end of Redlynch Intake Rd, to the west of the city centre. Basic picnic facilities are provided.

Cairns Beaches (p114, E1-D1)

Swimming isn't the first thing that springs to mind when you gaze upon the tidal mud flats along the city's waterfront. Indeed, the only place to swim here is **The Lagoon**, an attractive artificial 'water hole' and popular barbecue area on the foreshore at the end of Shields St. Don't despair, though, as a short drive to the north brings you to a series of beautiful palm-fringed swimming beaches backed by residential and holiday communities. Most have esplanades lined on one side by expensive apartments and motels, and on the other by narrow parklands with shady trees and picnic and barbecue facilities. All boast terrific views.

During the stinger season you can swim inside stinger-resistant enclosures at all the Cairns beaches. Palm Cove and Trinity Beach are patrolled by life-savers daily throughout the year, while the others are patrolled from September to May.

The first beach worth visiting is **Holloway Beach** with its popular little beachfront bar. At neighbouring **Yorkeys Knob**, 19km from Cairns, you can hire a charter boat to go fishing and diving, or cast off the rock wall at the entrance to the marina for barra and mangrove jack. The beach is a kiteboarding venue on weekends.

Trinity Beach, one of the most popular of the Cairns beaches, is next. It has better amenities than most, including several eateries clustered at the beach's northern end. At the other end is the 350m **Jack McKague Track**, which leads up to a lookout point with a nice view of the beach.

Continuing on, you come first to **Kewarra Beach** and then **Clifton Beach**. Both are quieter places, particularly Kewarra, which explains why neither have beachfront eateries. From Kewarra, Palm Beach sweeps northward in an unbroken crescent of sand all the way to Palm Cove.

Palm Cove, 26km from Cairns, is one of the region's more famous beaches and is fast becoming an important holiday destination in its own right. Cairns operators Big Cat, Compass, Quicksilver and Sunlover Cruises do island and/or reef trips from here, while Palm Cove Watersports (📞 0402 861 011) offers kayaking tours to nearby **Double Island**. Fishing off the jetty can yield mackerel, salmon and shark.

Cairns & Surrounds

Buchan Point is Cairns's unofficial nude beach but also a good spot to catch barra

Out on the Captain Cook Hwy, the **Cairns Tropical Zoo** (☎ 07 4055 3669) has a large collection of local wildlife and offers a variety of shows including feeding and photo sessions. There's also a night tour that includes entertainment and a torchlight tour looking for nocturnal wildlife (from $83).

After busy Palm Cove, a visit to nearby **Ellis Beach**, the final one in the series, is a welcome escape from the crowd – although it can get pretty busy itself on weekends. Along with Kewarra it's where the locals go to avoid the tourists. There are no housing estates or resorts here, just a caravan park, café and bar and grill. To the south of Ellis Beach, **Buchan Point** is Cairns's unofficial nude beach.

Where to Stay

Between them the Cairns beaches have a large slice of Cairns's holiday accommodation. However, budget places are only a little more common than hen's teeth and include the following:

- Billabong Caravan Park – Clifton Beach (☎ 07 4055 3737)
- Cairns Trinity Beach Holiday Park (☎ 07 4055 6306, www.trinitybeachpark.com.au)
- Ellis Beach Oceanfront Bungalows & Leisure Park (☎ 07 4055 3538, www.ellisbeachbungalows.com)
- Palm Cove Retreat Backpackers (☎ 07 4055 3630)
- Paradise Gardens Caravan Resort – Clifton Beach (☎ 07 4055 3712)

Islands off Cairns

Green Island (p114, E2)

Green Island, 27km northeast of Cairns, is probably FNQ's single most popular tourist attraction. The eastern half of this 12ha, picture-postcard coral cay is a national park covered in vine forest, while a resort occupies the remainder. It's extremely popular with Japanese visitors. The underwater observatory is a major attraction, and diving, snorkelling and glass-bottom boat tours are available. As most visitors congregate at the resort and adjacent

Cairns & Surrounds

Green Island

beaches, escaping the mob is simply a matter of taking the boardwalk through the forest to the other side of the island.

Getting There

The ferry ride from Cairns to Green Island takes about 45 minutes. Big Cat Green Island Reef Cruises (☎ 07 4051 0444) and Great Adventures (☎ 07 4044 9944) depart several times daily, charging $56 for the return trip. Big Cat also departs from Palm Cove.

Where to Stay

Green Island Resort (☎ 07 4031 3300, www .greenislandresort.com.au) offers a range of accommodation styles. Packages start at around $400 per room per night.

Fitzroy Island National Park
(p118, A2)

Named by Cook in 1770, this tall, rugged island of about 320ha is 29km southeast of Cairns, off Back Beach south of Yarrabah. It's a popular destination for day-trippers, who can indulge in a variety of outdoor pursuits. The **Fitzroy Island Resort** at the Welcome Bay ferry terminal offers kayak tours, snorkelling tours, dive tours (and courses) and glass-bottom boat tours. You can also hire catamarans, kayaks, fishing tackle and snorkelling gear. There are several walks including a climb to the island's highest point, where you're rewarded with a stunning panorama.

Arguably the island's major attraction is **Nudey Beach**, a pristine strip of dazzling sand about 10 minutes' walk from the resort. Despite the name, visitors aren't encouraged to reveal all.

Fitzroy Island's Nudey Beach

There's a fine view across to the mainland and good snorkelling around coral-encrusted boulders at the beach's northern end – visibility is at least reasonable even when the southeasterlies are blowing, as the beach is on the island's leeward side. Humpback whales are sometimes seen in the channel between the island and the mainland during their annual migration.

Getting There

Fitzroy Island is about 45 minutes by passenger ferry from Cairns. Day-trippers can get there and back with Fitzroy Island Ferries (☎ 07 4051 9588) and Sunlover Cruises (☎ 07 4050 1324). The return fare costs $36.

Where to Stay

The Fitzroy Island Resort (☎ 07 4051 9588, www.fitzroyisland.com.au) has bunkhouse beds for $31 and cabins from $72 per person.

Frankland Group National Park
(p118, B3)

Also named by Cook, the beautiful Frankland Group consists of several uninhabited small islands about halfway between Cairns and Innisfail. These densely forested, continental islands have a variety of land and shore habitats, making them good spots for bird-watching. The fringing reefs, particularly on the northern and western sides of **Normanby** and **Russell islands**, offer great snorkelling. Normanby Island displays characteristic features of both a tropical cay and a continental island.

Getting There

Frankland Island Cruise & Dive (☎ 07 4031 6300, www.franklandislands.com) runs day trips to the Frankland Group – a bus takes you from Cairns to Deeral, where you catch the boat. The day trip costs $129 including all activities such as walking and snorkelling tours guided by a biologist. The operator also provides a drop-off and pick-up service for campers but doesn't transport kayaks.

Experienced sea kayakers can access the Frankland Group from Deeral Landing on the Mulgrave River.

Where to Stay

There are QPWS campsites on High and Russell islands (☎ 13 13 04). ■

DENIS O'BYRNE

Cairns & Surrounds

Chapter Six

Atherton Tableland

Now marketed somewhat controversially as "The Cairns Highlands", the Atherton Tableland is a distinctive geographical unit less than an hour's drive southwest and west of Cairns. Much of its topography was shaped by volcanic activity that ceased as recently as 9000 years ago. At the time of White settlement the Tableland's rich basalt soils supported complex rainforest, but very little of this remains on the flatter areas.

The long-dormant volcanic vents are now filled with water and two of them – Lake Barrine and Lake Eacham – have become important nature-based tourist attractions. Built as part of an irrigation scheme, Lake Tinaroo has plenty to offer in the way of water sports such as fishing, canoeing, water-skiing and sailing. The surviving remnants of rainforest are home to many of the region's endemic fauna – wildlife spotting and walking are popular activities here. Hot-air ballooning and mountain biking are among the other things you can do.

The district's roads form a veritable maze, making it all but impossible to plan a route that doesn't require backtracking. All towns are accessible off the Kennedy Hwy (National Route 1), which runs through the heart of the Tableland between Cairns and Ravenshoe. You'll notice that, unlike the main coastal centres, towns on the Atherton Tableland have retained much of their early character. Herberton and Yungaburra are two places where historic walks are a major feature.

Mareeba (p117, A6)

On the Kennedy Hwy 64km from Cairns, Mareeba (pop 7000) was a major tobacco-growing centre until deregulation and anti-smoking campaigns put the farmers out of business. These days coffee is king along with crops such as fruit and vegetables, nuts, sugar cane and tea-tree oil.

The Mareeba Heritage Museum & Information Centre (℡ 07 4092 5674, www.mareebaheritagecentre.com.au) is at 345 Byrnes St.

What to See & Do

Scenic flights and hot-air balloon flights operate from Mareeba (see pp54-55) and the area has several nature-based attractions. The 2000ha **Mareeba Tropical Savannah & Wetland Reserve** (℡ 07 4093 2514, www.mareebawetlands.com) is off the Peninsula Developmental Rd about 14km northwest of town, and contains open savannah woodlands, grasslands, swamps and lagoons. This diversity of habitats makes it a good spot for bird-watching – 180 species have been recorded, of which 150 are seen on a regular basis.

TOURISM QUEENSLAND

Millaa Millaa Falls, evocative symbol of the Tableland

The reserve has a small captive flock of **Gouldian finches** that hopefully will one day be released into the wild. These richly coloured birds once occurred in great flocks right across northern Australia, including the Mareeba area. However, for reasons that are not yet fully understood, they have vanished from almost all their former haunts over the past few years.

You can hire canoes at the visitor centre, take a two-hour boat cruise or explore the various walking tracks. The latter range from 30 minutes to 2.5 hours and offer a variety of experiences. The reserve is closed during the Wet and at other times opens between 10am and 4pm Wednesday to Sunday inclusive and public holidays. Entry costs $8.

Granite Gorge (p117, B6) off Chewco Rd 9km southwest of Mareeba, features swimming holes and a 2.5km circuit walk through huge granite boulders. The gorge is noted for its rock wallabies, which can often be seen scrounging for handouts in the camping area.

Off the Kennedy Hwy between Mareeba and Kuranda, **Emerald Creek Falls** (p118, B1) in the Danbulla State Forest makes a delightful sight as it cascades over granite slabs and boulders on the dry western slopes of the Lamb Range. A 1km walking track takes you from the car park to a lookout above the falls. The 11km access road, which turns off the highway about 2.5km from Mareeba, is too rough for caravans. Picnic facilities are provided, and there are many small pools to cool off in.

Continue another 12.5km towards Kuranda and you come to the turn-off to **Davies Creek National Park** (p118, A/B1), The main attraction in this 5 sq km reserve is Davies Creek Falls, which offer a similar experience to Emerald Creek. You can camp here, but once again the access road is unsuitable for caravans. The base of the falls is a 2km boulder hop upstream from the camping area, while a car park 2km past the campground marks the start of a 1km circuit walk. There are some fine views from here.

The Davies Creek Falls car park is also a starting point for the strenuous day walk (return) to **Kahlpahlim Rock**, the highest point in the Lamb Range. This demanding exercise, which features breathtaking views over Cairns and the Tableland, is a 'must do' for walkers who enjoy a challenge. The Atherton QPWS office has a brochure, and the route is described in detail in the booklet *Tropical Walking Tracks: Cairns & Kuranda*.

Head southeast of town on Tinaroo Creek Rd – part of the Emerald Creek Falls access route – to the intersection of the Mt Edith and Kauri Creek roads. These roads join with the Danbulla Forest Drive (see the later section on Lake Tinaroo) to form a circuit called the **Tinaroo Range Road Network**. This is a good venue for 4WD and mountain-bike touring, with plenty of variety in topography and plant communities along the way. A QPWS "permit to traverse" is required to complete the circuit either by car or bike. Allow a full day if cycling.

DENIS O'BYRNE

Boat cruise in the Mareeba Wetlands

ROB VAN DRIESUM

Camping in Davies Creek National Park

Atherton Tableland

Where to Stay

Try the following budget places, all in town:

- Mareeba Country Caravan Park
  (☎ 07 4092 3081)
- Riverside Caravan Park (☎ 07 4092 2309)
- Tropical Tablelands Caravan Park
  (☎ 07 4092 1158)
- The Ant Hill Hotel (☎ 07 4092 1011)

Yungaburra (p118, C1)

Yungaburra (pop 1000) is off the Gillies Hwy 67km south of Cairns. This charming village was established in the early 1880s as a rest stop for diggers travelling between Cairns and the gold and tin fields further west. By the early years of the last century it had grown into a prosperous farming centre, but little has happened since then. The end result is an impressive collection of heritage-listed buildings, including a classic double-storeyed pub, the 1910 **Lake Eacham Hotel**.

Yungaburra is a short drive from the Crater Lakes National Park and the Danbulla Forest Drive at Lake Tinaroo. Other local attractions include wildlife tours and a popular country market held on the fourth Saturday of each month.

The visitor information centre (☎ 07 4095 2416, www.yungaburra.com) is on Cedar St near the hotel.

What to See & Do

You could easily spend the best part of a day in Yungaburra browsing through its craft shops and art galleries and doing the various walks on offer. The visitor centre has a leaflet that describes a self-guided walking tour of the town's heritage sites. You can tie this in with a stroll along Peterson Creek.

Starting on Mulgrave Rd, the easy 2.5km **Peterson Creek Walking Track** follows this little watercourse as it meanders past the western edge of town and under the Gillies Hwy. En route is a platypus viewing point at **Allumbah Pocket**, at the end of Penda St. If you're there at sunrise and sunset there's a good chance that you'll see one of these secretive animals. The Gillies Hwy Bridge is another platypus-watcher's hot spot.

From the bridge, a mown path heads west along the highway before veering left along the

Yungaburra Market on the fourth Saturday of the month is a very pleasant, laid-back event

The remarkable Curtain Fig

Atherton Tableland

verge of Fig Tree Rd. The destination for this walk is the **Curtain Fig**, a huge strangler fig in state forest about 2km from the bridge. It's a truly mind-boggling specimen and one that should sit high on the 'must see' list for any visit to the district. At night try spotlighting for green ringtail possums, coppery brushtails and Lumholtz's tree kangaroos.

Based in Yungaburra, Encounter Tours (☏ 07 4095 3532, www.encountertours.com.au) specialises in natural history and includes **Aboriginal culture walks** with a local indigenous elder. Alan's Wildlife Tours is also based here (see p34).

Where to Stay

There's quite a bit of accommodation in and around Yungaburra, including the following budget places:

- Lake Eacham Caravan Park – Lake Eacham (☏ 07 4095 3730, www.lakeeachamtouristpark.com)
- Lake Eacham Hotel – Yungaburra (☏ 07 4095 3515, www.yungaburrapub.com.au)
- Lakeside Motor Inn & Caravan Park – Tinaburra near Yungaburra (☏ 07 4095 3563)
- On The Wallaby Lodge – Yungaburra (☏ 07 4095 2031, www.onthewallaby.com)

ROB VAN DRIESUM

Lake Eacham

Crater Lakes National Park (p118, C1)

Crater Lakes National Park, off the Gillies Hwy near Yungaburra, consists of two volcanic craters filled with water and surrounded by complex rainforest in separate blocks about 2km apart. The craters, called *maars*, were created by explosions resulting from the superheating of groundwater.

Lake Barrine, the larger of the two, has a 5km walking track around its edge. Heading clockwise from the tearooms you soon arrive at two enormous kauris with an interpretive sign. Past here, keep an eye out for forest dragons and amethystine pythons sunning themselves at the water's edge. You may also see musky rat kangaroos feeding on the forest floor. Boat cruises operate on the lake from 10.15am, and travellers in the know try to avoid the hordes of coach passengers by getting on the first one.

Lake Eacham also has a circuit walk (3km) and is the most popular of the two lakes for swimming and picnicking. Over 180 species of birds have been recorded here, including 10 of the region's endemics.

The 'rape of the red cedar' in the late 19th and early 20th centuries almost wiped out this sought-after rainforest hardwood in FNQ. A rare and impressive survivor – simply called **The Red Cedar** – can be viewed at the end of a steep 300m path in Gadgarra State Forest, a short drive from Lake Eacham via Lakes Drive, Winfield Rd and Gadgarra Drive. It makes you wonder what this forest must have looked like prior to the introduction of steel axes.

Lake Tinaroo (p118, B1)

Lake Tinaroo was created in 1959 when a wall was built across the Barron River at Tinaroo Falls to provide water for irrigating crops in the Mareeba area. The lake is a short drive from Atherton and Yungaburra, and there are numerous places along the shore that can be reached in a conventional vehicle. Some of the most popular spots are accessible from the Danbulla Forest Drive.

What to See & Do

With over 200km of shoreline, much of which is lined by state forest, the lake is a major recreational playground for the Cairns region. Fishing, canoeing, water-skiing and sailing are

Atherton Tableland

popular activities, as are camping, picnicking and walking. If you'd rather not listen to the sound of speedboats zooming back and forth it might be best to visit on weekdays rather than weekends.

Danbulla Forest Drive

Starting at Tinaroo Dam, the 28km Danbulla Forest Drive passes through a mosaic of World Heritage rainforest, open eucalypt forest and softwood plantations within the 120 sq km **Danbulla State Forest**. As shown in the QPWS's excellent brochure *Forest Drive – Danbulla State Forest*, side roads lead into lakeside camping areas and points of interest including historic sites, rainforest walks, crater lakes and the majestic **Cathedral Fig**, a stunning tree well hidden in the forest.

Just past the Cathedral Fig car park, and about 250m from the end of the drive, a dry-weather track turns off across farmland to **Gillies Lookout** at 4km. A launching point for hang-gliders, the lookout offers magnificent views to the east.

The Danbulla Forest Drive terminates at the information shelter at the end of Boar Pocket Rd, and from here it's about 3km on a narrow sealed road to the Gillies Hwy near Lake Barrine. While the drive is well worth doing, you need to take extreme care as the road is often corrugated, narrow and dusty, with many blind corners. Kamikaze drivers are a hazard at all times, particularly on weekends and public holidays.

Fishing

Lake Tinaroo is kept stocked with a variety of fish, particularly barramundi, sooty grunter and sleepy cod. Some huge barra – including the world record – have been caught here, and there's no shortage of redclaw crayfish for entrée. Apart from Lake Koombooloomba near Ravenshoe, Lake Tinaroo is the only public water in FNQ where you can legally fish for barramundi all year round. A permit is required, however, and this can be purchased at various local outlets including the Atherton Post Office and the Lake Tinaroo Holiday Park.

Outboard-powered tinnies can be hired at Tinaroo (✆ 07 4095 8537), and guided fishing trips are also available (see p45).

Canoeing

Lake Tinaroo has many options, although windy conditions can generate waves of sufficient size to swamp a Canadian. The waters adjacent to the Kauri Creek and School Point camping areas are recommended for canoeing, but not for water-skiing. Someone should tell the skiers that!

Danbulla Forest Drive

Camping at Lake Tinaroo

Where to Stay

- QPWS Campgrounds – five bush camping areas scattered around the lakeshore within the state forest, all reached off the Danbulla Forest Drive, with basic facilities including tap water. Note that some sites must be pre-booked, which makes it imperative to sort things out in advance on ℂ 13 13 04.
- Lake Tinaroo Holiday Park on Dam Rd, Tinaroo – a range of accommodation a stone's throw from the lake (ℂ 07 4095 5232, www.ppawd.com/tinaroo)
- Tinaroo Tropical Houseboats – two to six-berth budget and luxury houseboats (ℂ 07 4095 8322, www.laketinaroo.com).

Atherton (p117, C6)

The second-largest town on the Atherton Tableland, Atherton is on the Kennedy Hwy 94km from Cairns. An early logging camp, it became a rest stop on the track between Port Douglas and the Herberton tin field. Today it has a population of around 6000 and is the commercial hub of the central Tableland.

Information

The excellent Atherton Tableland Visitor Information Centre (ℂ 07 4091 4222, www.athertonsc.qld.gov.au) is on the corner of Main St and Silo Rd. The QPWS office (ℂ 07 4091 1844) is at 83 Main St.

What to See & Do

Atherton and its near surrounds offer some good outdoor activities, including several bushwalks. Starting next to the children's playground on top of **Hallorans Hill**, a pathway leads down through a remnant patch of rainforest before terminating at Louise St (the road to Yungaburra). This particular type of forest, which is unique to the Atherton Tableland, has been all but wiped out. The walk is easy and enjoyable and takes about 30 minutes return. You can drive to the summit, which has landscaped picnic areas and a fine panoramic view over the Tableland.

With significantly more effort you get an even better view from nearby **Mt Baldy**, which overlooks Atherton from the southwest. To get there, take route 52 towards Herberton and turn off onto Rifle Range Rd just past the Piebald Creek Bridge on the edge of town. From here, follow the Gun Club signs for 700m to a small parking area at the track head. The walk is strenuous in parts, particularly the long, steep ascent to the first false crest! If you're feeling exhausted by then there's a bare area of rock where you can sit down and take a breather. Allow two hours to do the return walk, and do watch your footing on the loose stones and slippery slopes when heading back down.

Piebald Creek is home to several platypuses, and you might see one or two from the viewing point on the left of the bridge as you leave town.

Mt Bartle Frere seen from Hallorans Hill

Atherton Tableland

Continuing towards Herberton you soon come to the turn-off to **Hasties Swamp National Park**. Here the remnant of a once much larger wetland is one of the Far North's prime areas for viewing water birds. Over 220 species have been recorded, and a well-designed two-storey hide beside the road makes it easy to observe many of them.

About 8km from Atherton on the Kennedy Hwy towards Ravenshoe is the track head for the **Wongabel State Forest Botanical Walk**. This is an easy 2.6km circuit walk through a rare patch of the same type of rainforest found on Hallorans Hill. Plaques identify a large number of plants.

One of the more interesting relics of the volcanic activity that helped shape the Atherton Tableland is 16km further south in the **Mt Hypipamee National Park**. A well-made path leads 350m from the car park through the rainforest to what looks like a big sinkhole, but is, in fact, a type of **volcanic vent** called a diatreme. The vent, which was formed by the explosion of trapped, super-heated gases, drops sheer for 60m to what resembles toxic green sludge – actually a thick layer of pondweed. Below the weed it continues straight down for a further 80m, then turns under the lookout. Where it goes after that is a mystery.

From the crater lookout the track heads down through the rainforest to **Dinner Falls**, a series of small cascades on the upper Barron River. The forest, which is a high-altitude community of a type not found elsewhere on the Tableland, is home to Lumholtz's tree kangaroos and seven of Australia's 24 species of possums and gliders. Not surprisingly, it's a popular place for spotlighting.

Where to Stay

The following places are in town and won't blow your budget:

- Atherton Caravan Park (℡ 07 4091 1099, www.athertonvanpark.com)
- Atherton Hallorans Leisure Park (℡ 07 4091 4144, www.halloransleisurepark.com)
- Atherton Woodlands Caravan Park (℡ 07 4091 1407, www.woodlandscp.com.au)
- Atherton Travellers Lodge (℡ 07 4091 3552, www.athertonguesthouse.com.au)
- Hinterland Motel (℡ 07 4091 4807)
- Grand Hotel (℡ 07 4091 4899)

State-of-the-art bird hide at Hasties Swamp

Malanda Falls

Malanda (p118, C1)

Malanda (pop 1000) is a quiet, unassuming sort of place about 18km south of Yungaburra. The Malanda Falls Visitor Centre (℡ 07 4096 6957, www.cyberwizards.com.au/~malandafalls/) on the Atherton Rd has a wealth of information as well as interesting displays on the district's natural history, while the **Malanda Dairy Centre** offers an insight into the region's pioneering days.

Nearby, picturesque **Malanda Falls** plunges into a large pool surrounded by rainforest and lawns. There are a couple of short forest walks, one of which leads to a platypus-viewing platform, and the pool is a popular swimming spot. Ask at the visitor centre about **Aboriginal-guided walks** – guides were being trained at the

Atherton Tableland

time of writing. The friendly staff can also tell you about the best places to go spotlighting for wildlife such as possums and tree kangaroos.

South of Malanda on Upper Barron Rd, **Bromfields Swamp** is a permanent wetland in one of the Tableland's largest volcanic craters. This is another good spot to see water birds, and a viewing platform has been built for that purpose. Brolgas and sarus cranes are a feature from July to November, particularly in early morning and late afternoon.

The unique wooden dam wall at Irvinebank

Irvinebank, where time has stood still

Herberton (p117, C6)

Born out of a tin rush in 1880, Herberton (pop 1000) lies in attractive hilly country covered in open eucalypt forest, 19km south of Atherton. Mining ceased in 1978, leaving a legacy of yesteryear streetscapes that are well worth visiting for their own sakes. Indeed, the town's entire commercial precinct is listed on the Register of the National Estate. Also of interest is a 'historical village' made up of buildings that have been transplanted from other areas.

The Herberton Visitor Centre (☎ 07 4096 3474) at 47 Grace St has leaflets that describe 13 **walks** in and around the town. These range from 100m to 12km in length, with grades from easy to difficult. See the Bushwalking section on p30 for details of **donkey trekking** in the area.

Where to Stay

Budget options are limited, as are more expensive ones:

- Wild River Caravan Park (☎ 07 4096 2121)
- Royal Hotel (☎ 07 4096 2231)

Irvinebank (p117, C5)

Head west on the Herberton-Petford Rd for 28km – half of which is unsealed – and you come to the quaint little township of Irvinebank. Now home to around 100 people, Irvinebank was a tin-mining centre from 1882 to 1983 and many interesting relics of the early boom days remain. The National Trust has listed a number of the old buildings. If you've driven all this way you might as well have a look around – an expert guide can be arranged in advance by ringing the museum on ☎ 07 4096 4020.

Plant enthusiasts may want to make a beeline for Irvinebank to see the only species of wattle with purple flowers (*Acacia purpureapetala*) – in fact, it's reputed to be the only one without cream or yellow flowers. Visitors are encouraged to leave their secateurs at home.

Having sampled the pleasures of Irvinebank you can continue west for 26km to **Emuford**, another old mining centre. Among other things, you can view a historic ore-crushing plant and fossick for mineral specimens. Ring ☎ 07 4094 8304 for more information.

See the Savannah chapter for destinations further west.

Millaa Millaa (p118, D1)

Once famous for its cheese, this attractive little village is better known today for its waterfalls and scenic drives. The latter include the Waterfall Circuit; the new Palmerston Hwy to Innisfail (see p66); and the **Old Palmerston Hwy** from Millaa Millaa to the Kennedy Hwy – it intersects the latter between the Windy Hill Wind Farm and Ravenshoe. Neither the old highway nor the circuit drive are suitable for caravans.

The **Waterfall Circuit** (Scenic Route 9) follows Theresa Creek Rd as it describes a 14km loop off the Palmerston Hwy on the outskirts of town. This enjoyable short drive passes through a mosaic of steep cow paddocks and small remnants of rainforest. Detours en route lead in to picturesque **Millaa Millaa Falls**, **Zillie Falls** and **Ellinjaa Falls**, all of which flow over basalt cliffs in patches of rainforest. All three are readily accessible. Millaa Millaa Falls is a classic waterfall that drops into a deep

Pepina Falls

ROB VAN DRIESUM

Atherton Tableland

plunge pool. It's a popular swimming and picnicking spot.

There are several other waterfalls you can visit in this general area. **Mungalli Falls**, which drops 30m in three tiers, is the district's highest. It's on Brooks Rd off the Palmerston Hwy. Others of note are **Souita Falls** (on Middlebrook Rd off the Old Palmerston Hwy) – this one is well worth a look – and **Pepina Falls** (beside the Middlebrook Creek Bridge on the Old Palmerston Hwy).

The **Millaa Millaa Lookout**, off route 25 between Millaa Millaa and Malanda, offers inspiring views to the east, including Mt Bartle Frere if it's not in cloud.

Downtown Millaa Millaa

Give way to cows along the Old Palmerston Hwy

Ravenshoe (p117, D6)

Ravenshoe ("ravens-hoe", pop 900) lies off the Kennedy Hwy 56km south of Atherton and 150km from Cairns. Once a red cedar logging centre, this photogenic little township has an interesting geographical location. First, its elevation of 920m makes it Queensland's highest town. Second, it is right on the demarcation between the rainforests of the Tableland and the dry savannah country to the west. Ravenshoe's average annual rainfall is 1250mm – go 5km east and it increases to 1875mm, while 5km westwards it plummets to 625mm. Motorists heading west on the Savannah Way to Broome will find that Ravenshoe is the last town of any size in a long, long way.

Information

Ravenshoe has an excellent visitor centre (✆ 07 4097 7700, www.ravenshoechamber .com.au) on Moore St at the Kennedy Hwy end of town. The QPWS office is in the police station (✆ 07 4097 6721).

What to See & Do

There's quite a bit of potential for a nature-based holiday in Ravenshoe. Mt Hypipamee National Park and the Millaa Millaa waterfalls are about 25km to the north and northeast. Head west on the Kennedy Hwy for about 5km and you come to the turn-off to **Millstream Falls**. At 65m across it's said to be Australia's widest single-drop waterfall – which doesn't say much for the size of Australian waterfalls. An easy 300m walk leads down from the car park and picnic area to a viewing point.

Tully Gorge Rd heads south from town off the Kennedy Hwy into the Wet Tropics WHA and provides access to a number of attractions. This is a narrow rainforest road with many blind corners, so please drive carefully.

Two km down this road is the turn-off to **Little Millstream Falls**, a picturesque spot with a large plunge pool where you can – if very fortunate – see platypuses. Continue another 12km and you arrive at the first car park for the **Wabunga Wayemba Track**. This easy 6km circuit walk, which includes about 2km of roadway, is pure rainforest magic with a waterfall lookout and swimming hole thrown in. As the road is actually quite dangerous for walkers, it's recommended that you return to your car by walking back along the path.

Continuing south, the road passes track heads for sections of the **Misty Mountains Walks** (see the boxed text) before arriving at the **Tully Falls Lookout** turn-off, about 26km from the highway. There's an impressive view down into the 300m-deep gorge, but, because the water has been diverted for use in hydro-electric power generation, the falls only run during the Wet. A pleasant rainforest walk leads down to the top of the falls.

Tully Gorge Rd is sealed as far as the Tully Falls turn-off, after which it's mainly rough dirt for the remaining 19km to **Lake Koombooloomba** (p122, A1). Formed by a dam across the upper Tully River, this large rainforest impoundment is a popular spot for water-skiing, fishing for barramundi and black bream (no licence required), canoeing and camping. If you want to explore the forest roads in this area, you'll need 4WD or a mountain bike, plenty of experience and a QPWS "permit to traverse". One such route, often closed by washouts, goes via the Old Culpa Rd and Kirrama Station and eventually ends up at **Blencoe Falls** (see the boxed text on p60).

Places to Stay

The Tall Timbers Motel (☎ 07 4097 6325) out on the Kennedy Hwy has caravan and tent sites. ∎

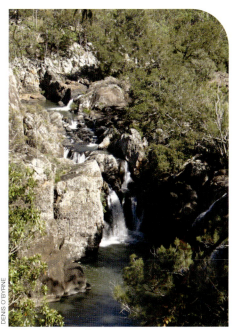

DENIS O'BYRNE

Little Millstream Falls

The Misty Mountains Walks

The mysterious Misty Mountains are made up of the rugged Cardwell and Walter Hill ranges between Tully, Innisfail and Ravenshoe. This remote area is noted for the diversity of its rainforest habitats and for its stunning landscapes. All of the region's endemic bird species are found here.

Few roads enter this magnificent part of the Wet Tropics WHA. However, for the bushwalker there is a network of eight high-altitude tracks that offer walks ranging from 7.5km (five hours) to 36km (30 hours) – several tracks can be combined to form a circuit in excess of 60km.

The walks total over 130km including detours. Several follow old logging roads that were constructed along the traditional routes taken by Aboriginal people as they travelled between the coastal lowlands and the Atherton Tableland. Each has its own outstanding attractions, whether these be unusual flora, particularly beautiful patches of forest, panoramic views, spectacular waterfalls or crystal-clear mountain streams gurgling over rocks.

During the Dry the various track heads are normally accessible to conventional vehicles except large camper vans. All walks are marked with coloured markers, and designated campsites – most without facilities – are provided at strategic intervals.

For more information on the Misty Mountains tracks, visit www.misty mountains.com.au. For an update on track conditions and road access, contact the QPWS office in Cairns on ☎ 07 4046 6600.

Atherton Tableland

Chapter Seven

Cairns to Cooktown

The coast road from Cairns to Cooktown takes you past – and through – some of FNQ's most beautiful country. Leaving the city centre it's 67km along the Captain Cook Hwy to Port Douglas, with some great coastal views en route (see Scenic Drives on p35-36).

From here it's only 20km to Mossman, where there's access to the southern end of Daintree National Park. The next stop is the Daintree River, where you kiss goodbye to the sugar cane plantations and say hello to the rainforest.

A cable ferry takes vehicles across the river on the 33km road to Cape Tribulation ("Cape Trib"). The road is like driving through a dimly lit green tunnel, with overhanging trees crowding close on either side. It is sealed as far as the cape, but it's narrow and winding and not recommended for large caravans. Watch out for cassowaries and oncoming traffic.

There's quite a bit on offer between the Daintree River and Cape Tribulation, and you could easily spend a week here if you wanted to see and do everything. Further north the tourist traffic drops right off, as the 30km between Cape Trib and the Bloomfield River is recommended 4WD only.

Beyond the Bloomfield River the track (now a 2WD road) continues through the Wet Tropics WHA until, at Black Mountain National Park, the rainforest gives way to dry eucalypt woodland. The road changes to bitumen and there's a rising sense of anticipation as you draw ever closer to Cooktown, one of the Outback's most alluring towns.

ROB VAN DRIESUM

The Bloomfield Track (left) and Cape Tribulation (above)

Port Douglas (p113, C6)

Originally called Island Point, Port Douglas leapt to prominence in 1877 when it became the shipping point for the Hodgkinson River Goldfield. Its growth was explosive and by 1879 it boasted 18 hotels and two newspapers. The town eventually declined to a quiet backwater, but saw renewed growth in the 1980s when it was the focus of major tourist developments such as Christopher Skase's Mirage Resort. Today it's one of the region's major tourist destinations, and despite rapid expansion has retained a wonderfully laid-back holiday atmosphere.

Port Douglas is handily located for day trips to Kuranda, Mossman, the Daintree River and Cape Tribulation.

Information

The Port Douglas Tourist Information Centre (℡ 07 4099 5599, www.pddt.com.au) is at 23 Macrossan St.

What to See & Do

Apart from wandering around the shops and drinking coffee in al fresco cafés, the major activity for holiday-makers at Port Douglas appears to be lazing about on beautiful, palm-fringed **Four-Mile Beach**. The beach is patrolled daily by life-savers and there's a netted swimming enclosure during the stinger season. Walk or drive up to the **Flagstaff Hill Lookout** for a nice view of the town and beach.

Turning off the Captain Cook Hwy onto Port Douglas Rd, you pass the **Rainforest Habitat** (℡ 07 4099 3235, www.rainforesthabitat.com.au) on the left. The large, walk-through aviaries are good places to see native birds that out in the jungle are often heard but very seldom seen. It opens from 8am to 5.30pm daily and entry costs $39/28 with/without breakfast – real fanatics can sit with the birds and share their muesli with them!

A 'must do' for hikers and mountain bikers is the legendary **Bump Track** (see the boxed text on p31). Bike N Hike (℡ 07 4099 4000) offers guided walks and rides along this route as well as rides along **Black Mountain Rd** (see the boxed text on p73).

Fishing is popular: you can hire tackle from Ship Shape (℡ 07 4099 5621) at 38 Wharf St.

Myall Beach at Cape Tribulation

ROB VAN DRIESUM

Four-Mile Beach at Port Douglas

DENIS O'BYRNE

Cairns to Cooktown

Easily accessible spots in and around town include the old Mowbray River Bridge, where you can try for the usual estuarine species. The rocks around Island Point yield barra, salmon, golden snapper, queenies and trevally. Outboard-powered tinnies are available for hire for fishing in Dixon Inlet, otherwise there's a swag of fishing charters (see pp44-45).

There are a number of **reef trips**. Among them, Wavelength (© 07 4099 5031) specialises in snorkelling tours, and there is whale-watching in season (see p47). Several operators visit the Low Isles.

Other activities include horse riding, hang-gliding, wildlife-watching, kayaking and kiteboarding – see the What to Do chapter for contact details. Most of Cairns's hot-air ballooning and white-water rafting operators do pick-ups in Port Douglas.

Where to Stay

Port Douglas has a few budget places mixed up with all the classy resorts, motels and holiday apartments:

- Dougie's Backpackers (© 07 4099 6200)
- Glengarry Caravan Park (© 07 4098 5922, 1800 888 134, www.glengarrypark.com.au)
- Pandanus Caravan Park (© 07 4099 5944)
- Port Central (© 0418 773 817)
- Port Douglas Backpackers (© 07 4099 4883)
- Port O' Call Lodge (© 07 4099 5422, www.portocall.com.au)
- Tropic Breeze Caravan Village (© 07 4099 5299)

Mossman (p113, C6)

The agricultural centre of Mossman, on the Captain Cook Hwy 75km from Cairns, appears to be totally unaffected by the tourist boom at nearby Port Douglas – probably because it isn't handy to a beaut beach. Still, there are a couple of things worth stopping for.

Mossman is 5km east of **Mossman Gorge**, a steep-sided valley in the rugged Daintree National Park. This is a popular picnicking area and active types can build up an appetite by walking the 2.7km **Rainforest Circuit**. Plaques along the way identify various tree species and reveal their traditional importance to local Aboriginal people. At the gorge, Kuku Yalanji

The ferry across the Daintree River takes you to a different world

Dreamtime Walks (© 07 4098 2595, www.yalanji.com.au) offers culture walks with the gorge's traditional custodians – recommended.

Mangrove Man Tours (© 07 4098 2066, www.mangroveman.com.au) specialises in the natural history of the **Mossman River**, particularly its mangroves.

The town of **Daintree**, 36km north of Mossman, is a centre for crocodile tours along the Daintree River.

The Daintree (p113, C6-A6)

The area known as the Daintree (not to be confused with the town of Daintree) is a 1200 sq km block of World Heritage rainforest that stretches from the Daintree River to near Cooktown. Much of it is mountainous, with elevations rising steeply from sea level to 1374m at Thornton Peak, one of Queensland's highest points. At Cape Trib the mountains come right down to the sea, creating some of the most outstanding scenery you'll see anywhere.

The Daintree River Ferry, at the end of a turn-off 26km north of Mossman, operates from 6am to 1am daily, crossing every 15 minutes or so. Motorists in the know get there early to avoid the queues.

Information

The Port Douglas Tourist Information Centre has quite a bit on the Cape Tribulation area. The fold-out 'maplet' issued with your ferry ticket is useful too. One of the best local places for advice is Mason's Store (© 07 4098 0070), on the main road about 2.5km south of Cape Trib.

The Bat House Environment Centre (© 07 4098 0063) at Cape Trib is the place to go for information on local environmental matters.

Cairns to Cooktown

What to See & Do

The Daintree rainforest is a major attraction due partly to the much-publicised confrontations between environmentalists and developers that have taken place here over the past 20-odd years. Many Australians who remember the bitter controversy that surrounded the construction of the Bloomfield Track will be curious to see what all the fuss was about.

Under a shady calophyllum tree at Cow Bay

Other-worldly mangrove forest at high tide, Marrdja Boardwalk

If you're at all interested in the natural processes that make up the Daintree eco-system, then the **Daintree Discovery Centre** (© 07 4098 9171, www.daintree-rec.com.au) should be your first stop. Its system of interpretive walkways, 23m-high canopy tower and lots of good information make for an absorbing experience. The turn-off is on the right about 10km past the ferry.

Virtually next door, the 700m **Jindalba Boardwalk** does a circuit through lush rainforest. It's worth getting here early to do the walk before the centre opens at 8.30am.

Back on the main road, the next major turn-off leads to **Cow Bay**. Here you find a delightful little beach contained between rocky headlands and fringed by coconut palms and shady calophyllum trees. It's the perfect place for a picnic lunch, and an excellent appetiser for the beaches further north.

Continuing past the **Ice Cream Factory** (great tropical flavours) you come to the **Fan Palm Boardwalk Café**. This place features an elevated walkway that meanders through dense jungle to terminate in an attractive stand of Licuala fan palms.

In the final 10km or so to the Cape the road passes three QPWS **interpretive boardwalks** that take you on a journey through the Daintree's evolutionary history – the **Marrdja Boardwalk** near Noah Creek is particularly worthwhile. Along the way are magical **Noah Beach** and **Myall Beach**. The **Cape Tribulation** settlement, which consists of a scatter of commercial buildings and accommodation places in the rainforest, is a short walk from the latter. Continue through the village to the **Kulki** day-use area at the southern end of Cape Tribulation Beach. This is where the reef trips depart, and there's a lookout with a good view of the beach and forest-clad mountains looming behind.

Keen bushwalkers will be tempted by this area's only fair dinkum walking track, the 7km return **Mt Sorrow Ridge Walk**. The track is often steep and difficult and takes at least six hours to complete, but the views from Mt Sorrow (650m) make it worthwhile. That's assuming of course that cloud hasn't settled on the ridge top. The track head is beside the main road about 150m past the Kulki turn-off – the sign is cunningly placed in a ditch and so is difficult to see.

ROB VAN DRIESUM

ROB VAN DRIESUM

Organised Tours

A number of boat cruises operate on the Daintree River and these leave from various points between the town of Daintree and the ferry. **Saltwater crocodiles** are a major attraction as the river has a large population of these prehistoric beasts.

Several operators are active between the Daintree Discovery Centre and Cape Tribulation. Heritage & Interpretive Tours (☏ 07 4098 7897, www.daintree-specialised-tours.com) has a day walk with a natural history bias. Mason's Tours (☏ 07 4098 0070, www.masonstours.com.au) has been around a long time and offers a range of treats including interpretive jungle walks, wildlife-spotting night walks, and 4WD trips on the Bloomfield Track. Cooper Creek Wilderness (☏ 07 4098 9126, walks@ccwild.com) and Jungle Adventures (☏ 07 4098 0090, www.jungleadventurescapetrib.com.au) also have guided day and night interpretive walks.

Other activities include specialised wildlife tours, fishing charters, scenic flights, horse rides, reef trips and sea-kayaking tours (see the What to Do chapter).

Where to Stay

There are quite a few places to stay along the main road, and you can pitch a tent at the following:

- Cape Tribulation Camping (☏ 07 4098 0077, www.capetribcamping.com.au)
- Crocodylus Village YHA (☏ 07 4098 9166)
- Lync-Haven Rainforest Retreat (☏ 07 4098 9155)
- Noah Beach Campground – pre-booked only (☏ 13 13 04)
- PK's Jungle Village (☏ 07 4098 0040, www.pksjunglevillage.com)
- Rainforest Village (☏ 07 4098 9015)
- Snapper Island – pre-booked only (☏ 13 13 04)
- The Jungle Lodge (☏ 07 4098 0034)

The Bloomfield Track

(p113, B6-A6; p111, D6-C5)

The first track through the Daintree was an Aboriginal footpath, later upgraded to a pack-horse track when White miners and settlers arrived on the scene. In 1968 a vehicle track was bulldozed through the rainforest between Cape Tribulation and the Bloomfield River, but the first wet season washed it away. Re-cleared a decade later, it soon became washed out and unusable once again.

In 1983 the Douglas Shire Council, supported by the state government, decided to construct a permanent road. Determined that the rainforest north of Cape Trib should remain untouched, environmentalists mounted a blockade that brought the area to national prominence. The road construction went ahead, but the publicity generated by the protest led to Queensland's wet tropical rainforests being listed as a World Heritage Area.

Today the 30km Bloomfield Track has been much upgraded, with creek crossings being improved and concrete laid on some of the steeper slopes. However, it's still not recommended for 2WD vehicles, mainly because of

ROB VAN DRIESUM

Noah Beach

Cairns to Cooktown

steep gradients (to 1:3) and resulting difficulties in maintaining traction.

The Bloomfield River crossing at Wujal Wujal used to be quite an obstacle but it has a concrete causeway now. Even so, great care is required whenever water is flowing over the causeway – there are no depth indicators, and saltwater crocodiles make wading across a risky undertaking. The causeway can be flooded either by rainfall run-off or high tides, or a combination of both, and the flow can be strong – wait until the water has subsided before proceeding. Check tide times at Cape Trib and Ayton.

Lion's Den Hotel, a good place for a break in proceedings

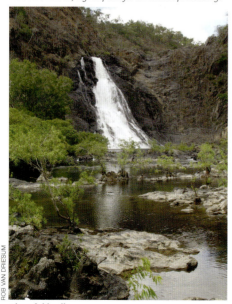

Bloomfield Falls

During the wet season the road can be closed for up to a fortnight at a time by flooded creeks and landslides. There are no facilities for travellers between Cape Trib and the Bloomfield River crossing, and only limited ones along the 74km between there and Cooktown.

Information

Mason's Store (℡ 07 4098 0070) at Cape Trib generally has up-to-date information on driving conditions. Its very useful *Cape Tribulation to Cooktown Map* includes distances, trip notes and driving tips.

What to See & Do

There's not a lot to see on the Bloomfield Track apart from rainforest, but the nature of the road makes the drive far from monotonous – particularly if it's been raining! At 22km from the Kulki turn-off, the **Woobadda River** has good swimming upstream from the crossing. Closer to the Bloomfield River causeway, Kuku Yalanji Rainforest Tours (Frances Walker, ℡ 07 4060 8069) offers **Aboriginal-guided cultural discoveries**, which are reputed to be very good.

At the northern end of the Bloomfield causeway, turn left to **Bloomfield Falls** (1.2km), a spectacular sight at the height of the Wet as the rain-swollen river plunges over a 40m drop. Back on the main road, the **CREB Track** to Roaring Meg Falls and Daintree Village is on the left, 2.3km past the causeway (see p37).

Tiny **Ayton**, 35km from Cape Trib, offers good fishing in the Bloomfield River, and you can take a charter or hire a tinnie from Bloomfield Boat Hire (℡ 07 4060 8252) at the river mouth. Its water taxi service visits beautiful **Cedar Bay** (only accessible by seaplane, boat or on foot) and **East Hope Island**, in the Hope Islands National Park. You can camp at both places, and the taxi service can arrange the necessary QPWS permits. Marine Air Seaplanes (℡ 07 4069 5915) in Cooktown will also take you there.

At Rossville, 24km from Ayton, you turn right for the **Home Rule Rainforest Lodge** (4km). This low-key bush resort includes a very attractive, park-like camping area on the banks of Wallaby Creek. The nearby water hole is the haunt of platypuses and the campground is a good spot to observe rainforest birds. There's a

ROB VAN DRIESUM

ROB VAN DRIESUM

Cairns to Cooktown

pleasant 2.5km return walk from the resort to some picturesque **cascades** complete with deep plunge pool.

The resort marks the beginning of a strenuous 17km walk through the rainforest to **Cedar Bay,** which boasts a remote and stunningly beautiful beach – allow two days for the return walk. The route description is included in *Tropical Walking Tracks (Port Douglas, Daintree & Cooktown).* Cedar Bay forms part of the **Cedar Bay National Park** and you'll require a QPWS permit to camp there.

Heading north once more, you soon come to the historic **Lion's Den Hotel**. This quintessential timber-and-iron bush pub is an excellent spot to wash the dust from your throat. You can swim in the creek, but ask at the pub first.

The intersection of the Bloomfield Rd with the sealed Cooktown Developmental Rd is 4km past the pub and 28km from Cooktown. A little further on, a roadside lookout offers a fine view of a mountainous pile of black granite boulders called – appropriately enough – **Black Mountain**. Actually the rock is grey – the black is algal growth. There's a sense of foreboding about the place, partly because of its rather eerie appearance and partly because of the legends that tell of people who've set out to explore it and never returned. The mount marks the northern end of the Wet Tropics WHA.

With 17km to go, you pass the turn-off to **Archer Point** (12km), which boasts great views from the lightstation at the end of the track, and a good, secluded beach camping spot down a track to the right, shortly before the open beach facing little Rocky Island. Ten km further along the Developmental Rd is **Keatings Lagoon**

Conservation Park, often a good spot to observe water birds late in the Dry. A 400m walking track leads around the edge of the wetland to a hide, and there's a picnic area 300m further on.

Where to Stay

- Bloomfield Cabins & Camping (℡ 07 4060 8207, www.bloomfieldcabins.com)
- East Hope Island – pre-booked only (℡ 13 13 04)
- Home Rule Rainforest Lodge – self-catering accommodation and camping (℡ 07 4060 3925)
- Lions Den Hotel rooms, cabins and camping (℡ 07 4060 3911, www.lionsdenhotel.com.au)

Black Mountain, an eerie place

Secluded beach at Archer Point

95

Palmer River Gold (p110, D2; p112, A2-B2)

When the Irish explorer James Venture Mulligan rode into Georgetown one day in September 1873 and put 102 ounces of nuggets from the Palmer River on public display, he sparked one of the wildest gold rushes Australia has ever seen.

At that time Georgetown, on the Etheridge Goldfield 300km southwest of present-day Cairns, was the closest settlement to the Palmer River. Being late in the dry season, water and game were scarce, and over 300km of harsh, trackless bush separated the two. Yet within days of Mulligan's find being made public, hundreds of men had left Georgetown and were following his blazed trail north to the Palmer.

By the end of October there were 600 diggers on the goldfield. The lack of rations had forced many to leave, but most of those who stayed on were doing well – some were getting up to five ounces a day, and 10-20 ounces per week was fairly common. Nuggets weighing up to 25 ounces had been found.

Not surprisingly, the local Aborigines resented this invasion of their land and the fouling of their water holes. They put up a stiff resistance and soon the diggers were finding it unwise to travel in groups of less than five. Eventually dozens of Whites and hundreds of Chinese were killed and whole tribes of Blacks were slaughtered in the name of Palmer River Gold.

The first wet season brought disaster to the 500 diggers who had delayed their departure too long. Trapped by flood waters many of them were reduced to eating boiled grass. Dysentery was widespread and soon the track to the brand new port of Cooktown was lined with graves. In Cooktown itself, over 2000 men sat around waiting impatiently for the rains to end. Many spent all their money in the pubs and brothels before they'd even set foot on the goldfields track.

Teamsters travelling to the Palmer from Cooktown had to take their wagons on a circuitous route of 270km across rough, difficult country. Still, it was worth their while as the going rate for cartage of a ton of goods was the equivalent of 40 ounces of gold. While the risks were great so were the profits, and wagons and draught animals changed hands for fabulous sums. The packhorse route was significantly shorter, but its narrow defiles were perfect spots for an ambush. Many travellers, particularly the poorly armed Chinese, lost their lives in Aboriginal attacks.

The peak year on the Palmer was 1875, with a recorded production of 250,400 ounces of gold. In its first four years it produced a recorded 40 tons of alluvial gold. Possibly as much again was smuggled out by the Chinese, who began to arrive in force in late 1874. Eventually their numbers peaked at 18,000 out of a total population of 24,000.

By 1880 the payable alluvial deposits had been worked out and a decade later the reef mines around **Maytown**, the principal settlement, were almost finished. Today nothing remains at Maytown apart from some paved street guttering, scattered rubbish and the replica of a typical miner's hut. It's hard to believe that in its heyday this was a 13-hotel town with a population of 10,000. Scattered through the surrounding hills are old reef mines whose steam-powered machinery, so laboriously transported in from Cooktown, is still largely intact. They make fascinating memorials to a colourful past.

Information

The Palmer River Resources Reserve, which includes many historic relics such as the Maytown site, is managed by QPWS rangers based in Chillagoe (℡ 07 4094 7163). Vehicle access is restricted to 4WD, and the usual route in is via the Whites Creek turn-off on the Peninsula Developmental Road (see p36). Other tracks lead in from Laura and Chillagoe.

The Palmer River in the Dry

Cooktown & Surrounds

(p111, B5/6)

Born of the Palmer River Gold Rush in 1873, "Cook's Town" grew rapidly to become Queensland's second-largest town and the busiest port outside Brisbane. At one time as many as 30,000 people lived there, and 94 hotels and numerous brothels vied to separate the diggers from their hard-won gold. However, boom was quickly followed by bust, and when the gold ran out, Cooktown went into a steep downward spiral until just 400 people were left. Today it's an attractive, sprawling place with a permanent population of about 1600 and a number of reminders of its boisterous beginnings.

Information

The official visitor information office is in the Cooktown Botanic Gardens (☏ 07 4069 6004, www.naturespowerhouse.com.au), on Walker St to the east of the CBD. Also check the town's official website, www.cooktown.com. The QPWS office (☏ 07 4069 5777) is on Webber Esplanade near the wharf.

What to See & Do

There are quite a few outdoor activities and nature-based attractions in and around Cooktown, including snorkelling, trail rides, bushwalks, fishing and camping.

The **Scenic Rim Walking Trail** is a circuitous route that connects Cooktown's historic buildings, Grassy Hill, the botanic gardens, Cherry Tree Bay and Mt Cook. If the visitor information desk at the botanic gardens doesn't have a map, the shire council office (☏ 07 4069 5444) in Charlotte St should. Otherwise get hold of *Tropical Walking Tracks (Port Douglas, The Daintree & Cooktown)*.

Cooktown has a number of interesting buildings and other relics that date from the 1870s and 80s, and these can be visited on a **historic walk** around the town area. They include the 1886 Bank of North Queensland building and the 1879 hospital – as fine examples of colonial architecture as you'll find anywhere in Australia.

The 60ha **Cooktown Botanic Gardens** – open daily between 9am and 5pm – has many displays of native and exotic plantings. Here too you'll find a display of magnificent botanical illustrations by the world-renowned artist Vera Scarth-Johnson. It's housed in the visitor centre, which also has quite a good café.

Cooktown's eastern side is dominated by 162m-high **Grassy Hill**, from where Cook was able to map out a course through the maze of reefs that barred his way offshore. The hill was covered in grass back then but the cessation of regular burning by Aboriginal people has allowed the bush to reclaim it.

ROB VAN DRIESUM

View out to sea from the summit of Cooktown's Grassy Hill

Grassy Hill's summit can be reached either on foot or by car and offers a fine view over the Endeavour River estuary and the nearby coast and ranges. Looking southwards, **Mt Cook** (431m) is the highest point on the horizon. There is no road to the top of Mt Cook but you can walk up from the edge of town. It's a strenuous climb through open eucalypt woodland and you should allow at least 2.5 hours to do the circuit.

Heading north from Cooktown on the Hope Vale Rd you come to the **Endeavour Falls Tourist Park** about 32km from town. Access to the falls, where a creek plunges over hexagonal-shaped columns of basalt, is through the van park. It's a good swimming spot.

Past Hope Vale the road eventually brings you to beautiful **Elim Beach** and **Coloured Sands**. Both are on land under the control of the Hope Vale Community Council (℡ 07 4060 9133), which charges $10 per vehicle per day to visit. Be careful not to be trapped by high tide. The Aboriginal-guided Guurrbi Tours (Willy Gordon, ℡ 07 4069 6022) will take you to significant rock-art sites in the Hope Vale area as well as teach you something about bush tucker and bush medicine.

Lizard Island National Park

About 100km north of Cooktown, Lizard Island National Park is made up of a group of six continental islands covered mainly by grassland and open eucalypt and acacia woodlands. Cook named **Lizard Island**, the largest in the group, in 1770 after the sand goannas he saw there. It offers wildlife-watching, walking tracks, postcard-perfect beaches and fringing coral reefs that are ideal for snorkellers. The view from **Cook's Look** (368m) – the island's highest point – is as sensational today as it was when Cook climbed the hill to spy a route out through the encircling reefs. Live-aboard dive boats visit from Cairns, with the potato cod in **Cod Hole** being a major attraction.

The Lizard Island Resort (℡ 07 4043 1999, www.lizardisland.com.au) has a range of packages starting at $765 per person twin-share. Otherwise there's a QPWS camping area (℡ 13 13 04) at the northern end of Mrs Watsons Bay, a 1.2km walk from the airport.

MacAir (℡ 13 1313) has connecting flights between Cairns and Lizard Island, while Marine Air Seaplanes (℡ 07 4069 5915) flies from Cooktown.

TOURISM QUEENSLAND

Lizard Island

Fishing

The best known fishing place in Cooktown is the **town wharf**, where Spanish mackerel, barramundi, bream and many more can be caught in season. It's a sight to behold when the Spanish mackerel are running, with anglers literally standing shoulder to shoulder for the full length of the wharf. You can imagine the fun and games when someone hooks a big one.

The old bridge over the **Annan River**, about 8km out on the Cooktown Developmental Rd, is reasonably consistent for barra, trevally, mangrove jack and bream. **Quarantine Bay**, about 8.5km by road south of town, can yield a variety of species such as whiting, flathead, trevally, mangrove jack and barra. The idea is to cast off the boulders north of the parking area at high tide. Despite the crocodile warning signs this is a popular swimming beach.

Further out again, casting off the old WWII groyne and wharf at **Archer Point** is worth a try for species such as barracuda, mackerel, trevally and queenfish. If they aren't biting you can at least enjoy some magnificent scenery! The 12km access road is unsealed – beware of gutters at creek crossings

Boat hire and fishing charters are available in the Cooktown area (see pp44 & 53). Marine Air Seaplanes (℡ 07 4069 5915) also offers fishing tours.

Where to Stay

Cooktown has a good variety of accommodation styles including caravan parks, B&Bs and a resort hotel. The following are budget places in and around town:

Cooktown

- Cooktown Caravan Park (℡ 07 4069 5536, www.cooktowncaravanpark.com)
- Cooktown Orchid Travellers Park (℡ 07 4069 6400)
- Cooktown Hotel (℡ 07 4069 5038)
- Peninsula Caravan Park (℡ 07 4069 5107, penpark@tpg.com.au)
- Pam's Place – backpackers (℡ 07 4069 5536, pamplace@tpg.com.au)
- Tropical Breeze Caravan Park (℡ 07 4069 5740)

Around Cooktown

- Endeavour Falls Tourist Park (℡ 07 4069 5431)

The Peninsula Developmental Rd between Lakeland and Laura

DENIS O'BYRNE

The Inland Route

Travellers lacking a 4WD vehicle can drive to Cooktown via the Peninsula Developmental Rd from Mount Molloy (p113, D6) to tiny Lakeland (p110, D4), then the Cooktown Developmental Rd from Lakeland to Cooktown. The only facilities on this 224km scenic route are at the Palmer River Roadhouse (112km) and Lakeland (143km). The Cooktown Developmental Rd should be fully sealed by the end of 2005.

From Lakeland there's a mostly unsealed detour of 62km to the little township of **Laura** (p110, C2). Fifty kilometres from Lakeland you come to the **Split Rock** art site, where faded paintings of human, spirit and animal figures in the distinctive Quinkan style decorate overhangs along a 4km circuit walk. Most visitors only go as far as the main gallery, which is about 250m from the car park. From here the track climbs the scarp to the top of the plateau, where it is poorly marked, and descends about 1km further on.

Quinkan art sites form part of the Aboriginal culture tours run by Steve Tresize of Jowalbinna Station (℡ 07 4060 3236), located 35km by 4WD road south of Laura. Two-hour to all-day tours are provided, and there's a good bush camping area at the homestead. The Quinkan Interpretive Centre (℡ 07 4060 3457) in Laura can provide details of Aboriginal-guided tours in the area. ∎

Cairns to Cooktown

Far North Queensland's western half is a vast, undulating ocean of eucalypt woodland that looks as if it hasn't changed much since the early days of White settlement. This is the eastern part of the savannah country that covers northern Australia from here to Broome. What towns there are tend to be very small, and most roads are unsealed. Travellers heading into the more remote parts of this region should be well prepared.

There are several worthwhile attractions. West of Mareeba are Chillagoe's striking limestone karst landscapes and cave systems, while the spectacular red scarp and mining history of Mt Mulligan can be discovered on a detour. Heading west from Ravenshoe on the Savannah Way you can see the amazing lava tubes in the Undara Volcanic National Park and check the gem fields near Innot Hot Springs and Mount Surprise.

West of Mareeba

Mt Mulligan (p112, E4)

The small agricultural centre of Dimbulah, on the Burke Developmental Rd 47km west of Mareeba, marks the turn-off to **Mt Mulligan Station** (© 07 4094 8360, www.outbackfarmstay.com.au) and one of FNQ's most dramatic landforms. Station owner Owen Rankine offers a variety of activities including guided walks, bush camping and horse rides.

Sometimes referred to as "Queensland's Ayers Rock", **Mt Mulligan** is an 18km-long ridge lined by rust-red sandstone cliffs that rise 400m above the surrounding country. The ridge is about 1km from the homestead, and between the two are the remains of the township that once serviced the old **Mt Mulligan Mine**. Coal was mined here from 1914 to 1957 – in 1921 Mt Mulligan was the scene of one of Australia's worst mining disasters when a horrific underground explosion killed the entire day shift of 75 men.

Mt Mulligan Station includes much of the **Hodgkinson River Goldfield** with its thousands of abandoned shafts and adits. Gold was discovered here in 1876 by JV Mulligan of Palmer River fame and soon there were 10,000 diggers on the scene. Several boom towns briefly flourished, **Thornborough** (p117, A5) among them. In its heyday Thornborough had a population of 1500 people and boasted several brick buildings and 22 hotels. For a time it was considered the capital of FNQ. However, it ultimately went the same way as its neighbours, leaving the cemetery and part of the Canton Hotel as its sole substantial relics.

Nearby is the historic **Tyrconnell Mine** (© 07 4093 5177, www.tyrconnell.com.au) (p117, A5), considered one of Australia's "finest and most complete examples of an early gold mine". Owners Andrew Bell and Cate Harley run tours of the 120-year-old crushing plant,

Mt Mulligan looms in the background

DENIS O'BYRNE

Mt Mulligan cemetery

DENIS O'BYRNE

and offer various activities such as bushwalks, evening cemetery walks and gold panning. On the other side of the ridge from Tyrconnell lie the scant remains of **Kingsborough** (p117, A5), the goldfield's second-largest town. A thousand people once lived here, but today the population comprises just the one resident – an expat Swede.

Getting There

Mt Mulligan is 50km north of Dimbulah – turn onto Stephens St – and all but the first 6.5km is unsealed. At 29km is the turn-off to the Tyrconnell Mine (5km) and Kingsborough (7km). Except during the Wet, when a 4WD vehicle is recommended, Tyrconnell and Mt Mulligan are accessible by conventional vehicle.

Where to Stay

Bookings are essential at all these places:

- Mt Mulligan Station – bush camping, homestead accommodation
- Tyrconnell Mine – camping and cabins
- Kingsborough – camping, budget rooms (🕿 07 4093 5955)

Chillagoe (p116, B3)

On the Burke Developmental Rd 136km from Mareeba, the quintessential outback town of Chillagoe (pop 200) was once famous for its huge smelting works. These days, however, tourism is all the go and the district's cave systems are the major attraction.

Access to Chillagoe from Mareeba is mainly by sealed road – only 23km is gravel. Coming from Undara it's a different story, with 122km of often rough dirt on the road via Sundown Outstation. The turn-off to Sundown is on the

Kennedy Hwy 50km from its intersection with the Gulf Developmental Rd (18km west of Mount Garnet).

Information

The Chillagoe Hub Information Centre (🕿 07 4094 7111, chillagoehubinfo@bigpond .com) on Queen St (the main thoroughfare) has interesting displays on the local geological and human history.

On Queen St opposite The Hub, the QPWS office (🕿 07 4094 7163) is the place to ask about self-guided cave tours within the national park.

What to See & Do

The main chimney of Chillagoe's old lead and copper **smelter** dominates the townscape. Now largely demolished, the smelter operated from 1901 to 1943 and enough remains to indicate that it must have been an impressive sight. The interpretive walk (or drive) around the site is worth doing even if you're not into industrial architecture.

There are three **show caves** – all in the Chillagoe-Mungana Caves National Park near town – and these can be visited daily on ranger-guided tours. Each has its own outstanding attractions – **Royal Arch Cave** features cavernous daylight chambers; **Donna Cave** has false floors and growths of cave coral; and **Trezkinn Cave** (only discovered in the 1960s) has some beautiful formations. A visit to all three costs $35.75 and you can get tickets at The Hub. They can be comfortably visited in a day, with tours starting at 9am (Donna Cave), 11am (Trezkinn Cave) and 1.30pm (Royal Cave).

In addition there are three undeveloped caves where you can do self-guided tours. **Pompeii** and **Bauhinia caves** are close to town near Donna and Trezkinn caves, while **Archway Cave** is about 15km out on the Burke Developmental Rd – there's an Aboriginal art site at the picnic area and car park. You don't have to be an experienced caver to explore these places, but you will need to take torches and wear old clothes, and some form of head protection is recommended. Archway Cave has plenty of variety and is the easiest cave to get around in, being mainly flat walking. Bauhinia Cave requires a reasonable level of fitness and agility, while Pompeii Cave falls somewhere in between.

DENIS O'BYRNE

The old Chillagoe smelter, still an impressive complex today

The Savannah

A 3.5km **walking track** leads from Royal Arch Cave to the Balancing Rock car park and from there it's a further 1km to the Donna Cave car park. This easy and enjoyable walk crosses **Chillagoe Creek** and meanders through striking karst formations. It's best done early in the morning to take advantage of the cooler conditions. **Balancing Rock** is a tall limestone column that balances on a narrow plinth – truly an amazing sight. It's accessed by a rough 400m circuit walk.

Where to Stay

For such a small town, Chillagoe has a good range of budget accommodation:

- Chillagoe Bush Camp & Eco Lodge – with star-watching at on-site observatory (℡ 07 4094 7155)
- Chillagoe Caves Lodge Caravan Park (℡ 07 4094 7106)
- Chillagoe Creek Homestead (℡ 07 4094 7160)
- Chillagoe Tourist Village (℡ 07 4094 7177)
- Post Office Hotel (℡ 07 4094 7119)

West of Ravenshoe

West from Ravenshoe on Hwy 1 are several highlights including Millstream Falls (see p86), gem fossicking around Innot Hot Springs and Mount Surprise, and the intriguing Undara Lava Tubes. One thing you'll notice almost immediately is the evidence of a dramatic drop-off in rainfall past Ravenshoe. In fact, within 5km of town the average annual rainfall drops from 1250mm to 625mm. No wonder the country looks drier!

Innot Hot Springs (p117, D5)

This tiny hamlet, 28km from Ravenshoe, is known for the therapeutic qualities of its thermal pools. The **Mt Gibson Fossicking Area**, 5km from town, is a good spot to look for gem-quality topaz (see p35).

Innot Hot Springs Village (℡ 07 4097 0136) has budget units and camping and van sites.

Forty Mile Scrub National Park
(p120, B4)

Straddling the Kennedy Hwy near the turn-off to the Undara Lava Tubes and Mount Surprise, this small park features a valuable remnant of the dry rainforest that once covered much of inland Queensland. Adrift on a sea of eucalypt woodland, the Forty Mile Scrub lies within a large area of basaltic country – the legacy of a long period of volcanic activity that ended about 190,000 years ago. Interpretive signs at an information shelter in the picnic area, and along a 300m circuit walk, tell you all about it.

DENIS O'BYRNE

Balancing Rock

ROB VAN DRIESUM

One of several marble quarries in the Chillagoe area

The Savannah

Undara Volcanic National Park

(p120, B3-C3)

The main attraction here is the **Undara Lava Tubes** – unusual geological structures that were created around 190,000 years ago when a volcano blew its top and sent lava streaming down the river beds that crossed the plain. As each river of lava flowed along, its outer surfaces cooled and hardened to form an insulating layer. This allowed the lava inside it to remain in a liquid state and so keep running until the tube was drained.

Today these large, tunnel-like structures – by far the world's largest of their type – can be visited on guided tours lasting two hours ($35), four hours ($65) and all day. The latter includes a walk around the rim of **Kalkani Crater** (not responsible for the tubes) with a good view of one of the lava flows. Contact Undara Experience (☎ 1800 990 992, www.undara .com.au) for bookings. Tours leave from the Lava Lodge (same contact details), which offers a range of accommodation including old railway carriages, safari tents and camping and van sites. Independent visits to the lava tubes are not allowed.

Other activities include several **self-guided walks** from the lodge's reception office, ranging from 2.3km to 12km. You can also drive to Kalkani Crater and do the 2.5km interpretive circuit walk around the rim.

Mount Surprise (p120, B2)

On the Gulf Developmental Rd 167km west of Ravenshoe, tiny Mount Surprise is the jumping-off point for visits to the **O'Briens Creek Gem Field** (see p35). O'Briens Creek is about 40km northwest of Mount Surprise

The partly collapsed lava tubes harbour patches of ancient dry rainforest in an otherwise harsh landscape

by unsealed road, and the turn-off is opposite the police station.

Mt Surprise Gems (☎ 07 4062 3055) has information about the field and hires fossicking equipment. You can whet your appetite by calling into the BP garage and checking the 3700-carat chunk of blue topaz found at O'Briens Creek in 1976.

Where to Stay

In Mount Surprise you'll find a couple of good caravan parks and a pub offering budget rooms:

- Bedrock Village (☎ 07 4062 3193, www.bedrockvillage.com.au)
- Mt Surprise Hotel (☎ 07 4062 3118)
- Mt Surprise Tourist Van Park & Motel (☎ 07 4062 3153) ∎

A massive lava tube in Undara Volcanic National Park

Index

Text & Atlas References

- **bold** page numbers – major text references
- normal page numbers – text references (minor references ignored)
- *red italics* – atlas references for places/ features mentioned in the text, specified by atlas page number followed by grid, e.g. "*113 C6*" means page 113, grid C6

Tully River

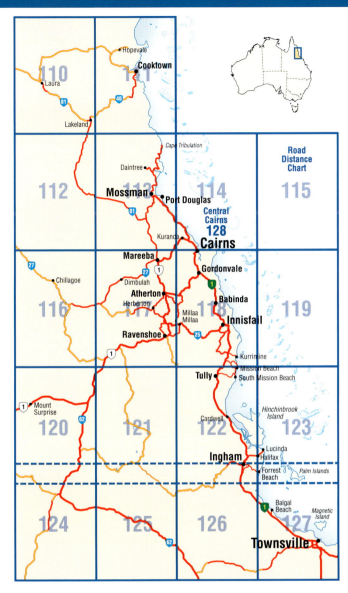

LEGEND

GPS-Plotted Roads & Tracks

Major Road	sealed	unsealed
Minor Road	sealed	unsealed
Track - 4WD only		
Rough Track		

Other Roads and Tracks

	sealed	unsealed
Major Highway	sealed	
Major Road	sealed	unsealed
Minor Road	sealed	unsealed
Track - 4WD only		
Rough Track		
Kilometres	100 / 50	
National Hwy/Route Number	A1 1	
State Route Number	62 A6	

Tourist Routes

Savannah Way/Alt. Route
Overlanders Way
Pacific Coast Way
Great Inland Way
Major Township • **Ingham**
Minor Township • Halifax
Aboriginal Community ◉ Wujal Wujal
Homestead • 'Weatherby'
Point of Interest • Scenic Railway
Parks/Reserves
Aboriginal Land
Defence Reserve
State Forest

Camping Area with facilities
Bush Camping
Roadside Rest Area with facilities
Roadside Rest Area with Overnight Camping
Lookout
Caravan Park/Caravan Sites
Operating Mine/Abandoned Mine
Alcohol Restrictions Apply
Information Centre
Airport; Airstrip/Airfield
24 Hour Fuel
Youth Hostel
Winery/Walking Track

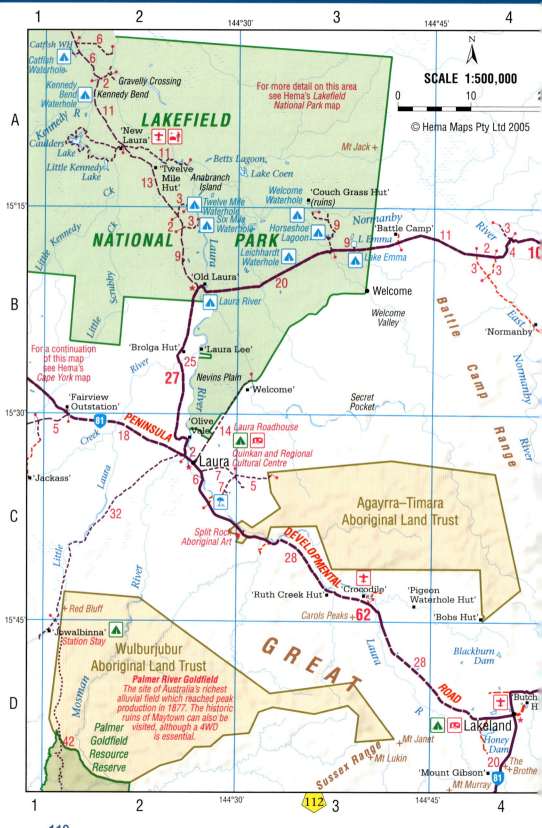

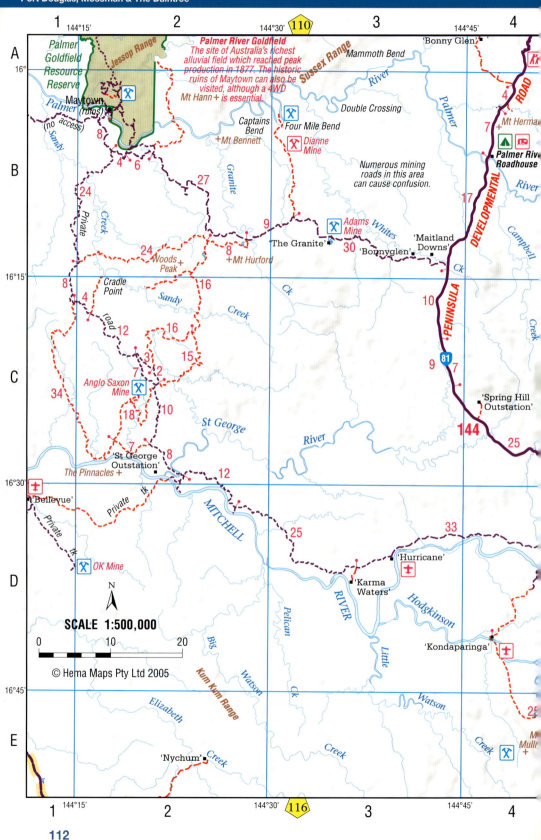

144°15' 144°30' **110** 144°45'

A
Palmer Goldfield Resource Reserve
Jessop Range
16°
Maytown (ruins)
Palmer (no access)
Sandy
Palmer River Goldfield
The site of Australia's richest alluvial field which reached peak production in 1877. The historic ruins of Maytown can also be visited, although a 4WD + Mt Hann+ is essential
Sussex Range
Mammoth Bend
River
'Bonny Glen'
ROAD
Mt Herma
Palmer
4
7
+

B
8
4 6
24
Private
Creek
27
Captains Bend +Mt Bennett
Four Mile Bend
Dianne Mine
Granite
9
The Granite'
Adams Mine
Whites
30
'Bonnyglen'
'Maitland Downs'
Ck
Numerous mining roads in this area can cause confusion.
Palmer Rive Roadhouse
17
DEVELOPMENTAL
River
Campbell

16°15'
8
4
Cradle Point
24
Woods + Peak
8
+Mt Hurford
16
Sandy
Creek
Ck
10
PENINSULA
Creek

C
34
12
16
16
3
15
7
2
Anglo Saxon Mine
18
10
St George
River
9 **81** 7
9
'Spring Hill Outstation'
144
25

16°30'
7
'St George Outstation'
The Pinnacles +
8
12
Bellevue'
Private tk
MITCHELL
25

D
Private tk
OK Mine
33
'Hurricane'
'Karma Waters'
RIVER
Hodgkinson
'Kondaparinga'

N
SCALE 1:500,000
0   10   20
© Hema Maps Pty Ltd 2005
Pelican
Little
Watson

16°45'
Big
Watson
Ck
Kum Kum Range
Elizabeth
Creek
Watson
Mulli +

E
'Nychum'
Creek
Creek
Creek
Mulli +

144°15' 144°30' **116** 144°45'

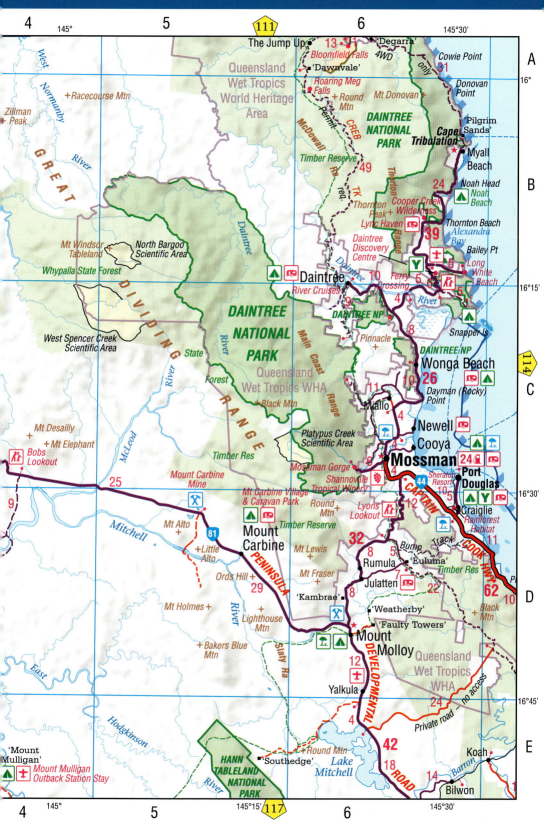

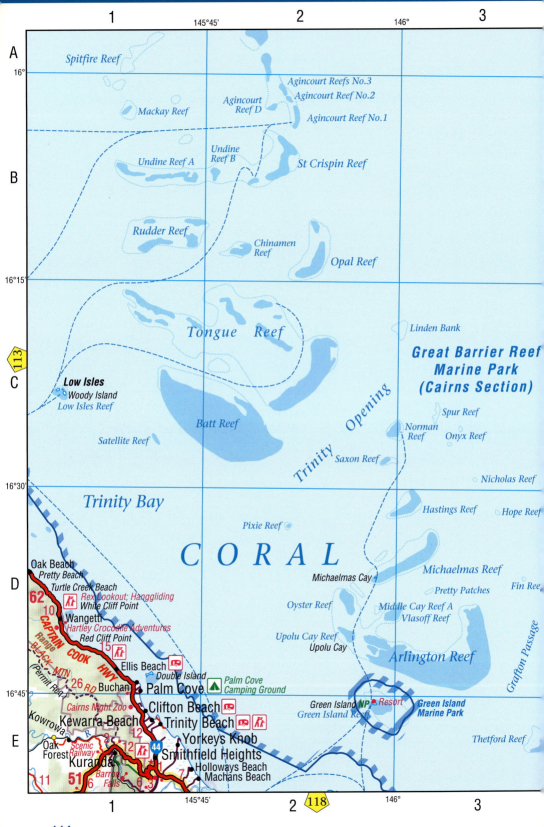

1   145°45'   **2**   146°   **3**

A

16°

Spitfire Reef

Mackay Reef

Agincourt Reefs No.3
Agincourt Reef No.2
Agincourt Reef No.1

Agincourt Reef D

Undine Reef A
Undine Reef B

St Crispin Reef

B

Rudder Reef

Chinamen Reef

Opal Reef

16°15'

Tongue Reef

Linden Bank

Great Barrier Reef Marine Park (Cairns Section)

113

C

Low Isles
Woody Island
Low Isles Reef

Batt Reef

Trinity Opening

Spur Reef

Norman Reef
Onyx Reef

Satellite Reef

Saxon Reef

Nicholas Reef

16°30'

Trinity Bay

Hastings Reef
Hope Reef

Pixie Reef

C O R A L

D

Oak Beach
Pretty Beach
Turtle Creek Beach
Rex Lookout; Hanggliding
White Cliff Point

62
10

Wangetti
Hartley Crocodile Adventures
Red Cliff Point

15

Ellis Beach
Double Island

Michaelmas Cay

Michaelmas Reef

Pretty Patches

Fin Ree

Oyster Reef

Middle Cay Reef A
Vlasoff Reef

Upolu Cay Reef
Upolu Cay

Arlington Reef

Grafton Passage

26 R.D.
Buchan

Palm Cove
Palm Cove Camping Ground

16°45'

44

Kowrowa
Kewarra Beach
Clifton Beach
Trinity Beach

Green Island NP *Resort*
Green Island Reef

Green Island Marine Park

Oak Forest
Scenic Railway
Kuranda

Yorkeys Knob
Smithfield Heights

Thetford Reef

E

9
12
12
11
7

Cairns Night Zoo

Barron Falls

51
6

11

Holloways Beach
Machans Beach

1   145°45'   **2**   118   146°   **3**

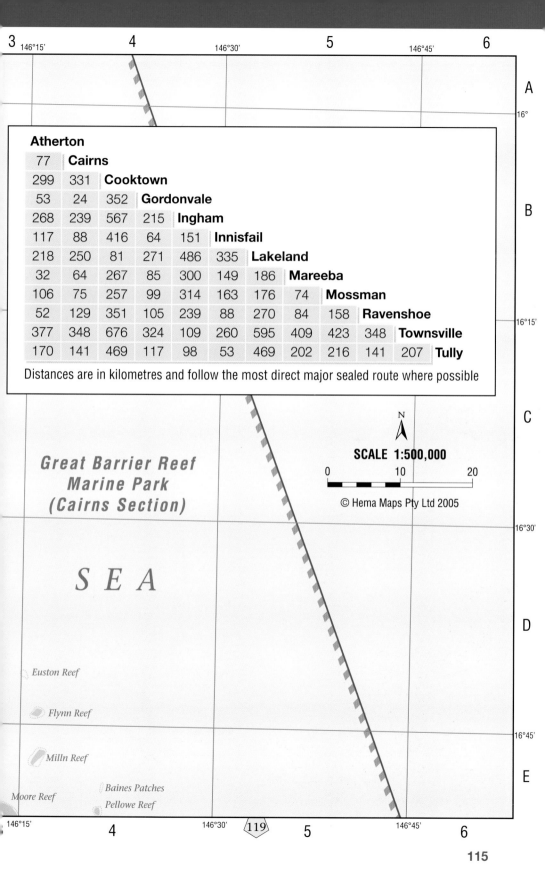

A

16°

Atherton

77	**Cairns**										
299	331	**Cooktown**									
53	24	352	**Gordonvale**								
268	239	567	215	**Ingham**							
117	88	416	64	151	**Innisfail**						
218	250	81	271	486	335	**Lakeland**					
32	64	267	85	300	149	186	**Mareeba**				
106	75	257	99	314	163	176	74	**Mossman**			
52	129	351	105	239	88	270	84	158	**Ravenshoe**		
377	348	676	324	109	260	595	409	423	348	**Townsville**	
170	141	469	117	98	53	469	202	216	141	207	**Tully**

Distances are in kilometres and follow the most direct major sealed route where possible

B

16°15'

N

Great Barrier Reef
Marine Park
(Cairns Section)

SCALE 1:500,000

0   10   20

© Hema Maps Pty Ltd 2005

C

16°30'

S E A

D

Euston Reef

Flynn Reef

16°45'

Milln Reef

Baines Patches

Moore Reef

Pellowe Reef

E

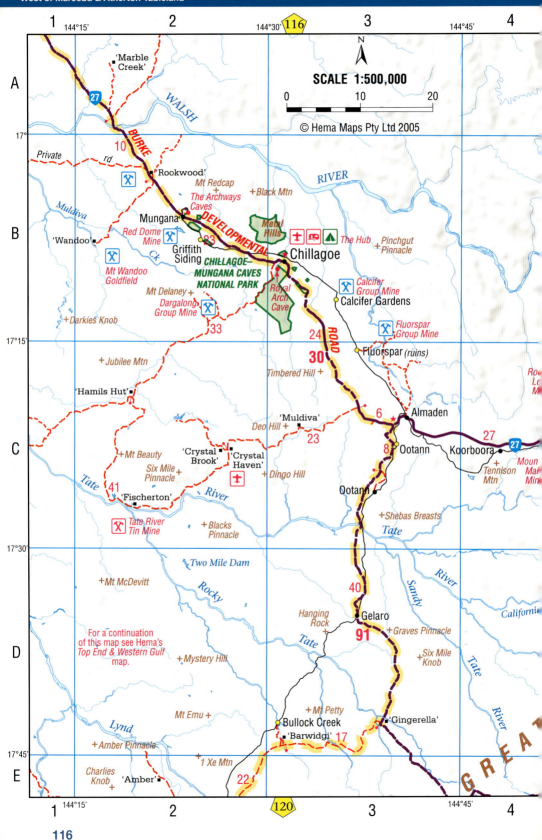

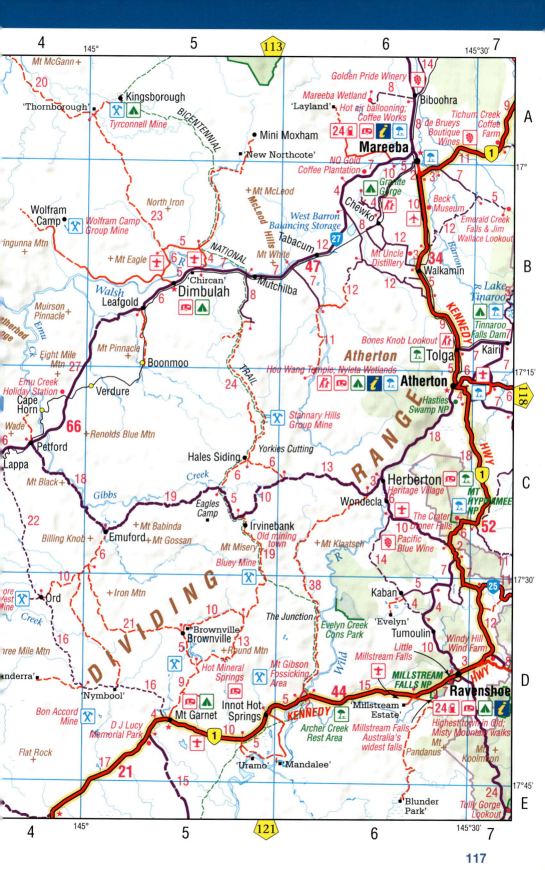

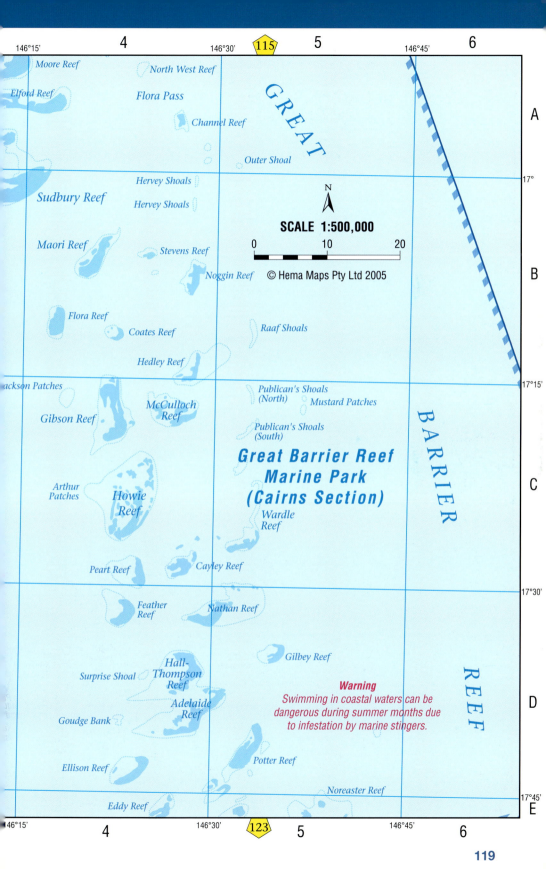

Moore Reef

North West Reef

Elford Reef

Flora Pass

Channel Reef

GREAT

Outer Shoal

A

17°

Hervey Shoals

Sudbury Reef

Hervey Shoals

N

SCALE 1:500,000

Maori Reef

Stevens Reef

0   10   20

B

Noggin Reef

© Hema Maps Pty Ltd 2005

Flora Reef

Coates Reef

Raaf Shoals

Hedley Reef

Jackson Patches

Publican's Shoals
(North)

Mustard Patches

17°15′

McCulloch
Reef

Gibson Reef

BARRIER

Publican's Shoals
(South)

**Great Barrier Reef
Marine Park
(Cairns Section)**

C

Arthur
Patches

Howie
Reef

Wardle
Reef

Peart Reef

Cayley Reef

17°30′

Feather
Reef

Nathan Reef

Gilbey Reef

REEF

Hall-
Thompson
Reef

Surprise Shoal

Warning

*Swimming in coastal waters can be
dangerous during summer months due
to infestation by marine stingers.*

D

Adelaide
Reef

Goudge Bank

Ellison Reef

Potter Reef

Noreaster Reef

17°45′

Eddy Reef

E

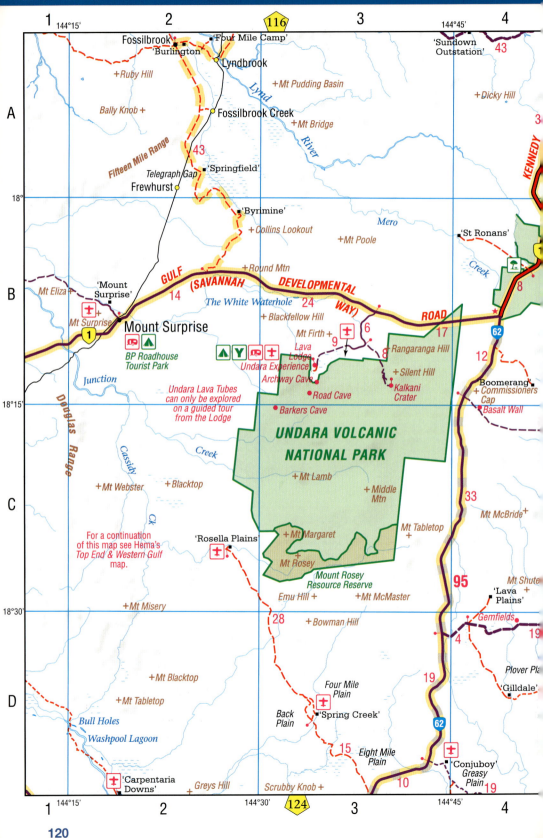

1 144°15'
2
3
4 144°45'

'Fossilbrook'
'Four Mile Camp'
Burlington
Lyndbrook
'Sundown Outstation'
43
+Ruby Hill
+Mt Pudding Basin
+Dicky Hill
Bally Knob +
Fossilbrook Creek
3
A
+Mt Bridge
Lynd River
Fifteen Mile Range
43
'Springfield'
Telegraph Gap
Frewhurst
'Byrimine'
Mero
'St Ronans'
18°
+Collins Lookout
+Mt Poole
Creek
+Round Mtn
8
Mt Eliza +
GULF (SAVANNAH
DEVELOPMENTAL
KENNEDY
B
Mt Eliza +
'Mount Surprise'
14
The White Waterhole
24
WAY)
ROAD
17
62
Mt Surprise +
+Blackfellow Hill
6
Mount Surprise
Mt Firth +
9
Rangaranga Hill
12
BP Roadhouse
Tourist Park
Lava Lodge
8
+Silent Hill
Boomerang
+Commissioners Cap
Junction
Undara Experience
Kalkani Crater
Basalt Wall
Archway Cave
18°15'
Undara Lava Tubes can only be explored on a guided tour from the Lodge
+Road Cave
+Barkers Cave
UNDARA VOLCANIC
33
Mt McBride +
Cassidy
Creek
NATIONAL PARK
C
+Mt Webster
+Blacktop
Douglas Range
Ck
+Mt Lamb
+Middle Mtn
95
Mt Shute
For a continuation of this map see Hema's Top End & Western Gulf map.
'Rosella Plains'
+Mt Margaret
Mt Tabletop +
'Lava Plains'
+Mt Rosey
Mount Rosey Resource Reserve
Gemfields
18°30'
+Mt Misery
28
Emu Hill +
+Mt McMaster
4
19
+Bowman Hill
Plover Pla
+Mt Blacktop
19
+Mt Tabletop
Four Mile Plain
Gilldale'
D
Bull Holes
Back Plain
'Spring Creek'
62
Washpool Lagoon
15
Eight Mile Plain
10
'Conjuboy' Greasy Plain
'Carpentaria Downs'
+Greys Hill
Scrubby Knob +
19
1 144°15'
2
3 144°45'
4

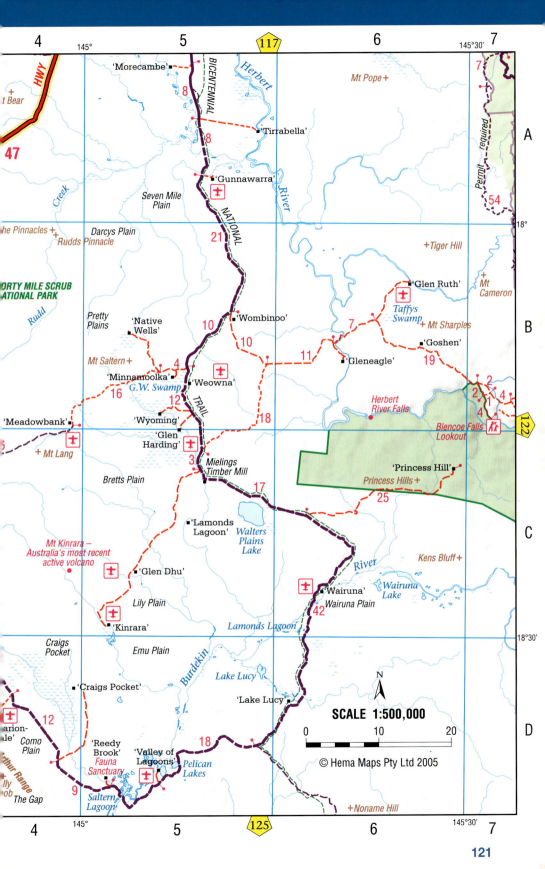

Farquarson Reef

Noreaster Reef

Beaver Cay

Taylor Reef

radise Estate Wines;
ysses Link Walking Track

Beaver Reef

Yamacutta Reef

G R E A T

Moss Reef

Dunk Island Spit

18°

B A R R I E R

Otter Reef

Barnett Patches

Kennedy Shoal

Duncan Reef

Brook Islands
North Island

Shepherd Bay

Cape Sandwich
Eva Island

Britomart Reef

18°15'

Ramsay Bay

**Great Barrier Reef
Marine Park
(Central Section)**

Nina Peak
Mt Bowen
1121m

Agnes Island

Trunk Reef

Thorsborne Trail
(Bookings essential)

Zoe Falls   Zoe Bay

Mt Diamantina

Mulligan Falls

Hillcock Point

Bramble Reef

Hinchinbrook
Fish Habitat
Area

Mulligan Bay

George Point

Rib Reef

18°30'

House boat hire

RRINGUN NP   Dungeness
Lucinda

R E E F

Macknade   5.7km long sugar
loading facility

Pelorus Island
(North Palm Island)
(Yanooa Island)

Iris Point

Halifax

Cordelia

Halifax Fish
Habitat Area

Little
Pioneer
Bay

Orpheus Island
(Goolboddi)

N

SCALE 1:500,000

Taylors Beach

Yanks
Jetty

NATIONAL PARK
Orpheus Island Resort

0   10   20

Harrier Pt
Fantome
Island (Eumilli)

Curacoa Island
(Noogoo)

Sunballa Point

© Hema Maps Pty Ltd 2005

Lady Elliot Reef

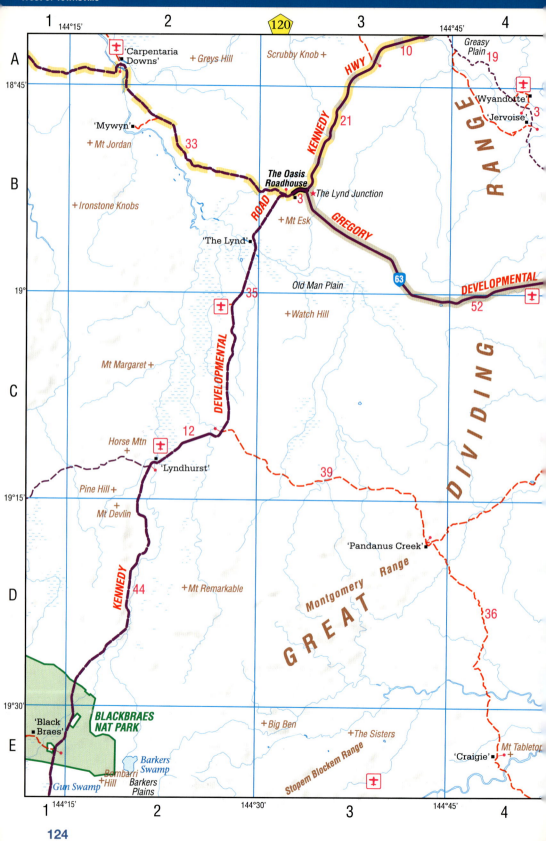

144°15' 120 144°45'

1 2 3 4

A
'Carpentaria Downs' + Greys Hill Scrubby Knob + HWY KENNEDY 10 Greasy Plain 19
18°45' Wyandotte Jervoise 3

'Mywyn' 33 21
+ Mt Jordan

B + Ironstone Knobs ROAD The Oasis Roadhouse 3 ★ The Lynd Junction GREGORY RANGE
+ Mt Esk
'The Lynd' 63 DEVELOPMENTAL
19° Old Man Plain 52
35 + Watch Hill

Mt Margaret + DEVELOPMENTAL DIVIDING

C
Horse Mtn 12
+ 'Lyndhurst' 39

Pine Hill +
19°15' + Mt Devlin 'Pandanus Creek'

Montgomery Range

D KENNEDY 44 + Mt Remarkable GREAT 36

19°30' BLACKBRAES NAT PARK Big Ben + + The Sisters
'Black Braes' Mt Tabletop
E Barkers Swamp Stopem Blockem Range 'Craigie' +
Bambarri Hill + Barkers Plains
Gun Swamp

144°15' 144°30' 144°45'
1 2 3 4

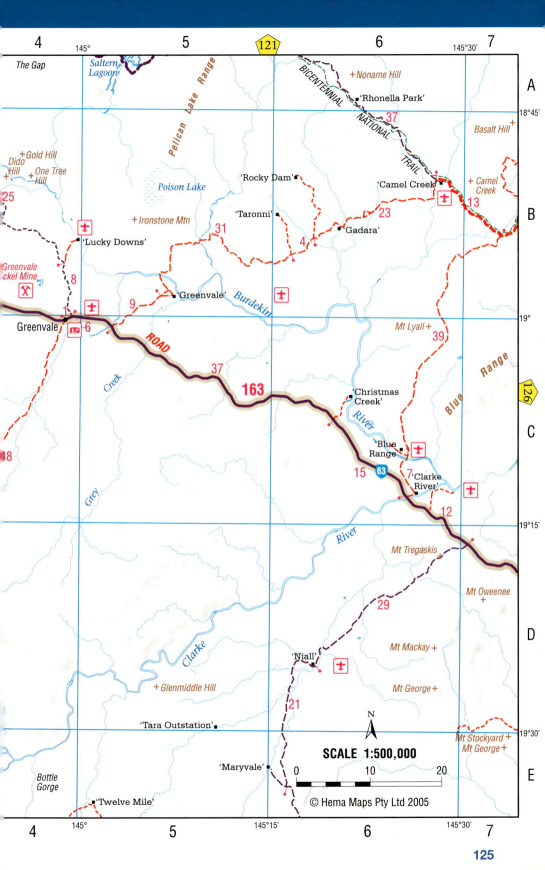

145°   145°30'

The Gap

Saltern Lagoon

Pelican Lake Range

+ Noname Hill

BICENTENNIAL NATIONAL TRAIL

'Rhonella Park'

A

18°45'

37

Basalt Hill +

Dido Hill +
+ Gold Hill
+ One Tree Hill

Poison Lake

'Rocky Dam'

'Camel Creek'

+ Camel Creek

25

+ Ironstone Mtn

'Taronni'

23

13

B

Greenvale ckel Mine

8

31

4

'Gadara'

Lucky Downs'

9

'Greenvale'

Burdekin

Mt Lyall +

39

Greenvale

6

ROAD

37

163

'Christmas Creek'

River

Blue Range

Range

C

19°

18

15   63

'Blue Range'

7 'Clarke River'

12

Creek

Grey

River

Mt Tregaskis

19°15'

Clarke

29

Mt Oweenee +

'Niall'

Mt Mackay +

Mt George +

+ Glenmiddle Hill

21

'Tara Outstation'

Mt Stockyard +
Mt George +

19°30'

N

'Maryvale'

Bottle Gorge

SCALE 1:500,000

0   10   20

'Twelve Mile'

© Hema Maps Pty Ltd 2005

126

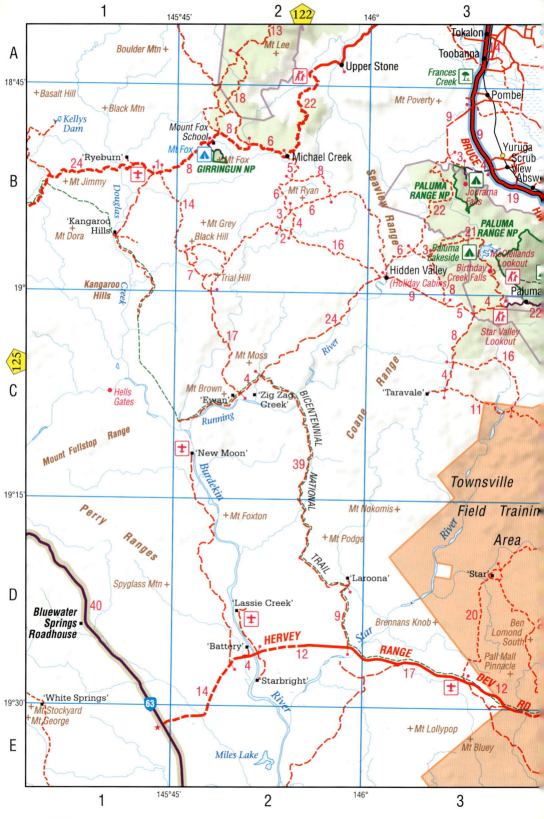

Palm Islands
Great Palm Island

Ladt Elliot Reef

Forrest Beach

Cassady Beach
Palm Creek
Cons Park

Palm Creek
Fish Habitat Area

Bronte
Beach

Fantome
Island
(Eumilli)

Palm Island

Sunballa Point

+ Mt Bentley

Electra Head

South West Cape

Esk Island
(Soopun)

Brisk Island
(Culgarool)

Pandora Reef

A

18°45'

Cattle Creek
Fish Habitat Area

HALIFAX BAY WETLANDS NP

Havannah
Island

N

SCALE 1:500,000

0   10   20

© Hema Maps Pty Ltd 2005

B

Halifax Bay

Coolbie

Barrilgie

Mutarnee

Moongobulla

Acheron Island

Cordelia Rocks Reef

19°

Little Crystal
Creek Bridge

le View

Mtn+

Rollingstone
State Forest

A1

Balgal Beach

Lorne Reef

Herald Island

Rattlesnake
Island

PALUMA
RANGE NP

109

Rollingstone

Toomulla

21

Toomulla
Beach

Paluma
Shoals

Magnetic Island
NAT PARK

Bungalow
Bay YHA

C

Paluma
State
Forest

Mt Halifax

Clemant
State Forest

Toolakea

Jalloonda

Bluewater

Bohle River
Fish Habitat
Area

West Point

HorseShoe
Bay

Y

Arcadia
Bay

Nelly Bay

Picnic Bay

35

Yabulu
Refinery

BRUCE

Yabulu

Black River

Mount
Low

Townsville
Town Common
Cons Park

Pallarenda

*Cleveland
Bay*

19°15'

'Ponto
Hut'

Annaville

30

Nightjar

Deeragun

Ferry

HWY

24

Y

i

Townsville

RANGE

DEV

10

RD

Douglas

Ognoonba

Cluden

HERVEY

19

Alice River

Rupertswood

12

Bohle Plains

Rasmussen

Kelso

James Cook
University

Stuart

A1

Julago

D

Pipers
Lookout

'Narraweena'
Ben Lomond East

Ben Lomond
West

'Table
Top'

'Camp
Guilfoyle'

'Camp
Engstrom'

+Frederick
Peak

Mount Stuart
Defence Res

Brookhill

Big Jack
Oak Valley

FLINDERS

Alligator
Creek

Antill Plains

Alligator
Creek

11

Range Control

Round Mtn+

Grasshopper Range

22

133

Townsville

Field Training

Area

Ross River
Dam

A6

HWY

Toonpan

+Pepper Pot Mtn

BOWLING
GREEN BAY
NAT PARK

19°30'

E

To Northern Beaches, Port Douglas and Mossman

To Airport and Jack Barnes Bicentennial Mangrove Boardwalk

Scale 1:22,000

N

Saltwater Creek

CAIRNS HARBOUR

CAIRNS NORTH

EDGE HILL

Walking Tracks Rainforest
Lookout
Red Arrow Circuit

McCormack St
Stuart St
Goodwin St
Flecker Botanic Gardens
Macdonnell
Queenley Cl
The Tanks

Collins Av
Rainforest Boardwalk
McLean St
Sheridan St
Seymour St
Moffat St
O'Keefe St
Howe St
Rutherford St

Greenslopes St
Centenary Lakes
McLeod St
Short St
Arthur St
Cairns North School
Hockey Grounds
Tobruk Memorial Gardens & Pool

Police Citizens Youth Club
Watsons Park
Revival Centre Church
Lily St
Cairns St
Smith St
Digger St
Lake St

North Cairns A.F.L.
Cemetery
John St
Edward St
McKenzie St

Behan St
Macnamara St
Marine Radio Club
SES
Hollett Cl
Lane
Thomas St
McLeod St
Charles St
Digger St
Little Charles St
Grove St
Esplanade

Anderson St
Adelaide St
Donaldson St
Fearnley St
Chaplain Av
Severin St
Teatree Cl
James St
Martyn St
Shearer St
Thomas Av
Charles St
City Council Depot
Gelling St
Bert St
Charles St
Cairns Base Hospital
Kerwin St

Wilkinson St
Mylchreest St
David St
Brisbane St
Queen St
Denbeigh St
Draper St
Parramatta St
Dunn St
Martin St
McLeod St
Gatton St
Cairns State High School
Upward St
Calvary Hospital
Minnie St
Grafton St

PARRAMATTA PARK
Trinity Bay High School
T.A.F.E. College
Newton St
Fallon St
Eureka St
Roseblank St
Grove St
Upward St
Pembroke St
Balfe St
Severin St
Harris St
Clare St
Archie St
Mary St
Nellie St
Water St
Maranoa St
Florence St
Munro Martin
Lake St
Abbott St
Esplanade
"The Pier" Shopping Centre
Lagoon
The Domain

Monk St
Bowls
Gatton St
Aumuller St
Collinson St
Jones St
Buchan St
Gregory St
Minnie St
Road
Miller St
Warrego St
Cairns Central Shopping Centre
McLeod St
Aplin St
Sheridan St
Shields St
City Mall
i
CAIRNS
Reef Fleet Terminal
Marlin
Cairns Reef Casino
Radisson Plaza

Veivers Cl
Boland St
Curtin St
Creed St
Mann St
Vivian Cl
Hector Cl
Hogan St
Brown St
Earl St
Hannam St
Ascot Av
Mulgrave Rd
Showground Shopping Centre
Quigley St
Bunting St
Winkworth St
Parramatta Primary Sch
Parramatta Park
Victoria St
Loeven St
Scott St
Barlow Park Sports Centre
St Augustine's
St Joseph's School
Bunda St
Grimshaw St
Terminus St
Jubilee St
Robb St
Draper St
Palm Av
Lumley St
Taylor St
Spence St
Police HQ Courthouse
Cairns Convention Centre
Wharf St
Hilton Hotel
Cairns City Council Offices
Cairns City Council Offices
Trinity

West Court Shopping Plaza
O'Leary St
Doyle St
Allan St
Barrett St
Edgar St
Frederick St
Wellington St
Joan St
Spence St
Morehead St
Kidston St
Ogden St
Buchan St
Plath St
Fearnley St
Owen St
Hartley St
Central St
East St
Kenny St
Police Cl
Trinity Inlet

To Gordonvale and Innisfail